EROTIC ART OF SHIBARI

MASTER JAPANESE ROPE BONDAGE TO ENHANCE INTIMACY, INTENSIFY SEXUAL FULFILLMENT, DEEPEN CONNECTIONS, BUILD TRUST, AND EMPOWER SELF-DISCOVERY

THAT ROPE GUY

TABOO PRESS

CONTENTS

INTRODUCTION

I am **That Knot Guy**. In this book, I will guide you and your partner to go on an enriching exploration of the captivating world of Shibari. Whether you purchased this book or received it as a thoughtful gift, I invite you to momentarily set aside any preconceived notions and embark on this journey with an open and receptive mind.

Background

Before delving deeper, let's take a moment to explore the history of the intricate art of Japanese rope bondage.

Japanese culture boasts a rich history of rope use in various contexts. Traditionally, rope played a role in sacred rituals and was also employed in martial arts, specifically Hojojutsu, for restraining defeated adversaries or crimi-nals. The complexity of the ties varied greatly, often reflecting one's social standing and how well respected you are as a person. Shibari, the focus of this book, represents a more contemporary adaptation of rope art, primarily in an erotic context. While it likely draws inspiration from Hojo-jutsu, that is where the similarities end. Images of rope bondage first emerged in Japan in the 1920s and later became a staple in the adult magazine 'Kitan Club.'

In recent years, Shibari has gained global recognition, appreciated both as a BDSM activity and a form of both erotic and artistic bondage, which places a strong emphasis on the aesthetic, emotional, and sensual aspects of rope tying. More importantly, it symbolizes deep trust and intimacy between partners, transcending physical restraint to encompass emotional and spiritual bonding.

I first heard about the practice of using rope to tie up women for sexual gratification at too young of an age. It wasn't until much later in life, however, that I finally got any real exposure to it...and I have been hooked ever since. Its exquisite aesthetics and the profound intimacy it fosters have captivated me. Now, I hope to ignite the same passion for this unique form of artistic expression within you.

About This Book

This is my second book on the topic of rope bondage. The aim is to introduce you to the art of Shibari. If you've never been a Boy Scout, a sailor, or only have limited exposure to common knots, I highly recommend you to read my first book, <u>Knot Tying 101: The Ultimate Beginner's Pocket Guide to 7 Most Useful Knots You Will Ever Need for Shibari</u>. However, prior experience is optional for mastering the ties detailed in the following pages. The illustrations and step-by-step instructions offer sufficient guidance to easily follow along.

As you flip through the pages of this book, you will likely notice some topless photos throughout the chapters. Please note that you do not need to practice bondage on a nude or semi-nude model. Any ties could be performed on fully or partially clothed individuals if that is your preference. However, I had an opportunity to add some beautiful imagery to illustrate the ties, and obviously, I went for it. Without being overly sexist, the world could use more beautiful forms in print (to simplify, tit pics never hurt anyone).

This book is your invitation to navigate the art of Shibari, designed to enhance intimacy and deepen the connection between you and your partner. This book is meant for anyone interested in Shibari. It welcomes all individuals of any gender, pronoun, sexual orientation, or identification. Authored and illustrated by yours truly, That Rope Guy, and with the invaluable collaboration of my fantastic rope partner, the lovely @naughty1andsexy1, we often refer to 'her' for relatability in both illustrations and text. However, we want to assure our readers of all pronouns and gender identification that roles are fluid, and you may choose to be on either end of this connection.

As you go forward, you will make choices along your path. You can choose to take control or give it up ... but you could also try both sides by switching your role each time you play. This will allow you to get a glimpse into a different perspective. Provided that you and your partner have fully negotiated and agreed on how you will play ahead of time, there is no wrong way to do Shibari.

When working on this book, I aimed to avoid creating an overly complicated guide full of rigid instructions. Instead, my goal is to show the vast possibilities that the realm of bondage holds for you, the reader. I want to instill in you the confidence to embark on an intimate journey with your partner, elevating your bedroom game to an entirely new level. Above all, let's not forget the crucial element of enjoyment—because, let's face it, exploring the world of bondage should be nothing short of fun!

My goal is to show you the rabbit hole. It's up to you to see how deep down the hole that rope will take you and which turn you want to take. So, take your first wrap and enjoy the journey!

What You Will Need

2-3 hanks of rope[1], approximately 26 feet long each - I used handmade jute rope for illustrative purposes throughout this book, but feel free to use what you like or whatever rope type you might already have.

- If you are like me and enjoy that traditional look synonymous with Shibari and the feel of natural fiber, you might want to use jute or hemp. Though both are considered natural fibers, they do "handle" differently, so you must try them to determine which one you like better. In recent years, I have also seen bamboo rope being used. Finally, in some rare cases, one might be allergic to natural fiber. For those individuals, a good alternative would be cotton rope.

- Alternatively, you might use nylon rope. For me, synthetic rope offers the advantages of having many vivid color options, being washable, and, more importantly, since it is machine-made, it provides consistency in construction (thereby its strength). The disadvantages are that the smoother texture makes it less grippy (so the knot will come undone more easily) and more prone to causing rope burn if you pull the rope against the skin too quickly. I've included a selection of photos at the conclusion of chapters 1 and 4, featuring the use of nylon rope to visually highlight this material's distinct aesthetic.

Safety shears - Always have a pair of safety shears within reach while practicing Shibari. They are inexpensive and readily available. They can be purchased at local pharmacies, big box retailers, and online stores.

Remember

The common practice is to fold the rope in half, thus working with the double rope. The curved section formed on one side where the rope is folded is called the "**bight**," while the loose or opposite end is called the "**working end**." (I will reference these terms throughout this book, so please keep the above definitions in mind.) Most people (including me) will start each tie with the bight end after folding the rope in half, but if you find starting with the loose end fits your style better, go for it. One advantage of starting a tie with the working end is that you will always finish with the bite and thus will avoid finishing with two ropes of different lengths. The downside is that your options for tie-off become more limited. If you do extension(s) during a tie, you will need to form the lark's head at the end of the rope, which might be a little awkward (that is, until you get used to it).

All the ties were performed with a rope originally cut to around 8m long. Over time, ropes tend to stretch, so their lengths may not remain precisely the same. With that being the case, and depending on your partner's flexibility, physique, or any other unique physical attributes, most likely, your ties will not look exactly like the ones shown on the following pages. And that's perfectly fine. What truly matters is the intimate connection formed and the quality time spent together.

Consent and safety

Shibari is a beautiful art form that demands respect for its beauty, complexity, and potential risks. Safety and consent are first and foremost in rope bondage. Prioritizing safety ensures the well-being of both parties involved. At the same time, continuous and enthusiastic consent fosters a sacred space where you and your partner can embrace vulnerability within the preset boundaries. **Remember, practicing Shibari requires your partner's active and ongoing consent.**

Please remember that just because you have seen cool ties in photos or videos does not mean you should try them on your partner without proper training or precaution.

When practicing Shibari, always prioritize all participants' safety and well-being through good communication. Most importantly, **always** use common sense:

1. Practice any new knots or variations in controlled settings before using them on your partner. (you can always try it on yourself, if possible.)
2. Have a pair of safety shears within reach while practicing Shibari. They are inexpensive and readily available. They can be purchased at local pharmacies, big box retailers, and online stores.
3. Test knots to ensure they are adequately secured and can hold the intended load before relying on them during play.
4. Make sure to dress a knot properly. In addition to being aesthetically pleasing, it ensures the highest strength for the knot.
5. Ensure that the tie is not too tight. Check for proper circulation and ask your partner if it is sustainable. A general rule is to make sure two fingers can go under a tie
6. Adjust the tightness of the wraps or knots if necessary, ensuring your partner's well-being.

---

1. *A "hank" of rope refers to a coil or loop of rope wound or twisted in a specific way, often for storage or transport. This coiling allows the rope to be stored neatly without tangling, making it easier to use when needed.*

1

———

BASIC CHEST HARNESS

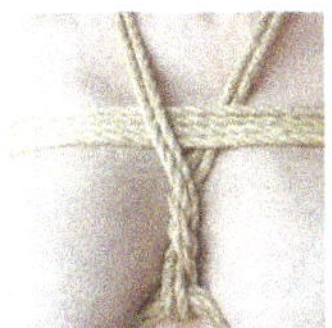

Chest harnesses in Shibari are not just functional; they are deeply symbolic. Traditionally, these harnesses were designed to restrict movement and to symbolize capture and control. However, in the modern context of Shibari, they have transcended these origins to become a form of intimate art. The design of these harnesses varies from simple patterns to intricate weaves that require hours to perfect.

I have selected this basic chest harness to initiate your journey into rope play. It balances ease of learning and the opportunity to exercise control and artistic expression while fostering a deeper connection with your partner. Its simplicity allows quick learning and application, making it suitable even in the most spontaneous moments. This tie is ideal for those who prefer a simpler approach over elaborate knotting and intricate weaves. Furthermore, once you complete the first 8 steps, I will provide a couple options to utilize any extra rope, offering further creative possibilities to exercise control during bedroom play.

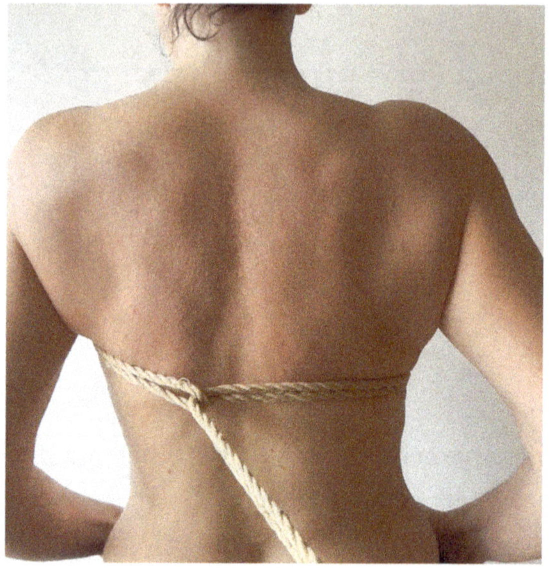

Step 1: Start your chest harness with a lark's head above your partner's breasts. Wrap the working end in the opposite direction to create two bands of rope above your partner's chest.

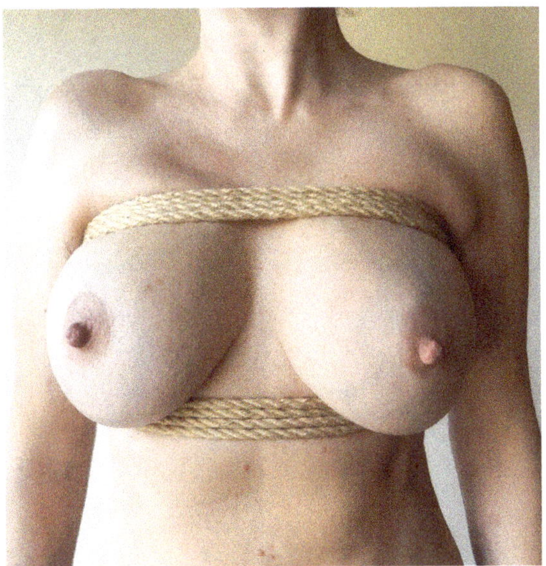

Step 2: Form two bands of rope underneath the breasts as well.

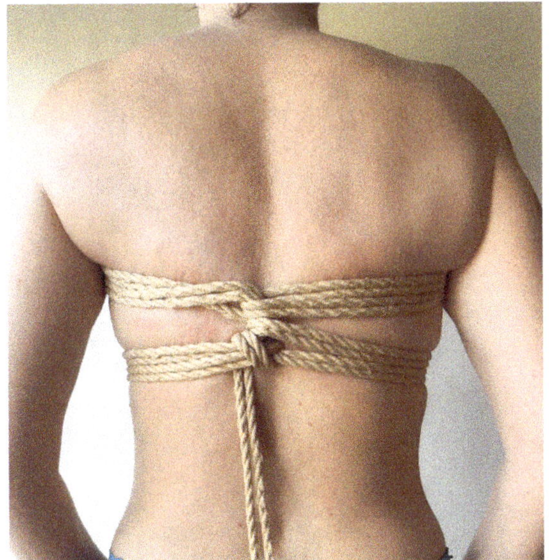

Step 3: Tuck the working end under the bottom band from the top and pull it down.

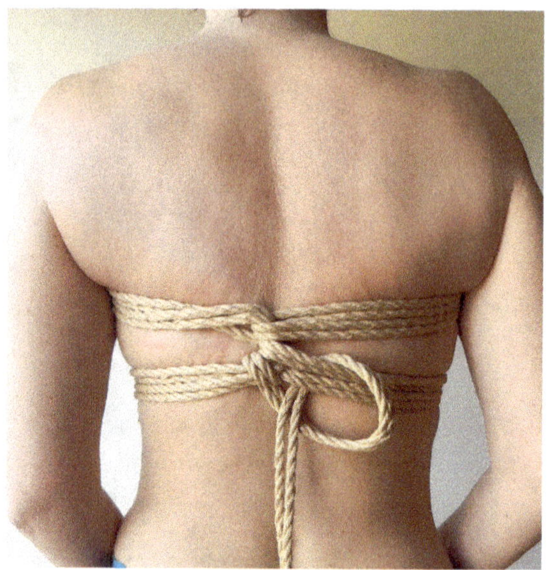

Step 4: Lock off the tie by creating a half hitch, as shown.

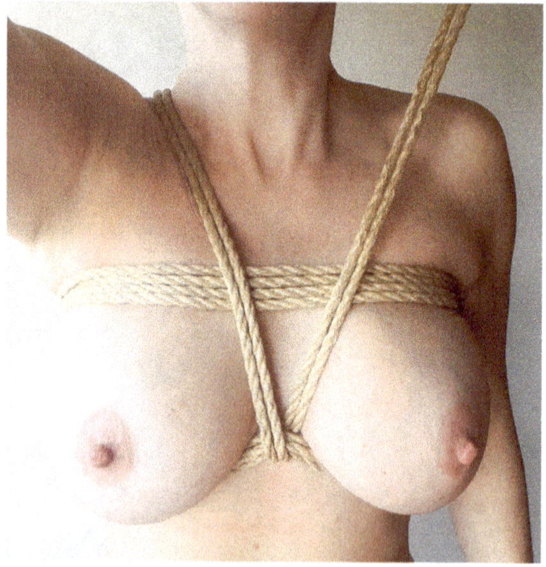

Step 5: Pull the working end up over the right shoulder and tuck it under the bottom band.

Note: Adding this V-shaped detail helps to restrain the movement of the bottom horizontal bands, preventing it from sliding downward.

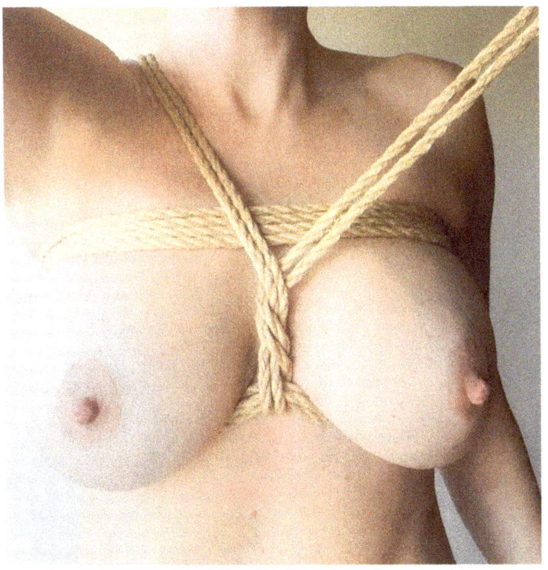

Step 6 (Optional): To add some additional visual details to the tie, wrap the working end a couple times around the strap, as shown.

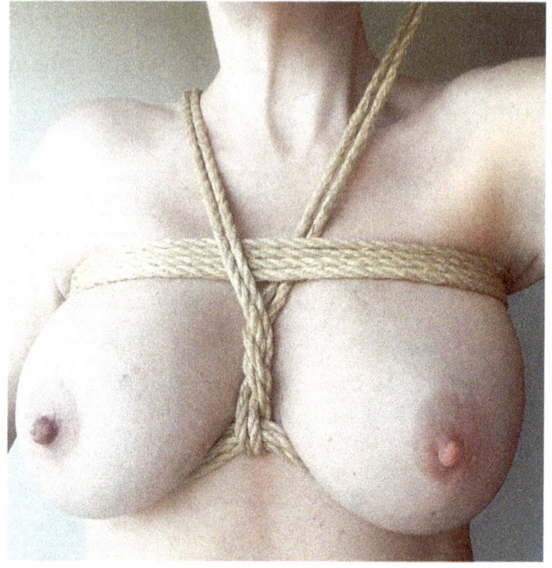

Step 7 (Optional): Tuck the working end under the top band before bringing it over the left shoulder.

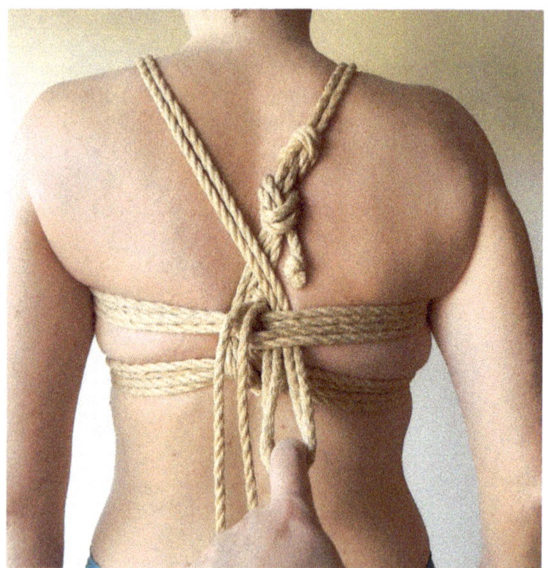

Step 8: Tuck the working end under the top band on the right side and pull through

At the end of Step 8, you have completed your basic chest harness. Now, you just need to do a tie-off to prevent the chest harness from coming undone.

However, if you have extra rope left and want to do something with it. Here are some options:

Option A - Creating a Leash/chain

You can use the remaining rope to create a "rope chain" to be used as a leash. The chain can be a loose chain or a tighter chain. As you follow the next few steps, keep in mind that smaller links create tighter chain whereas larger links create looser one.

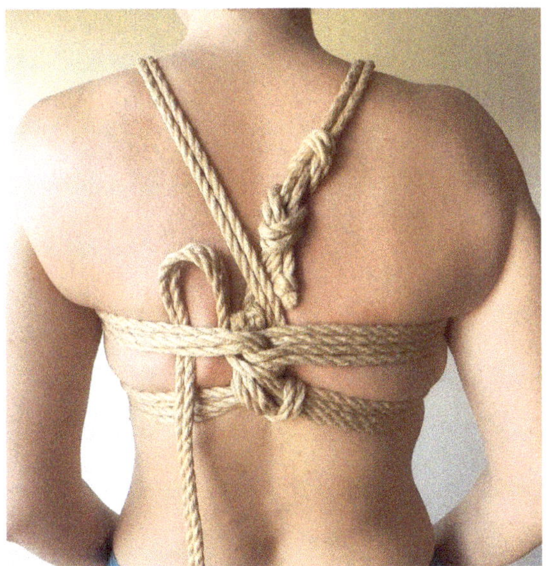

Step 9: Fold the working end to create a bight and bring the bight up from behind on the left side. This bight becomes the loop needed for the next step.

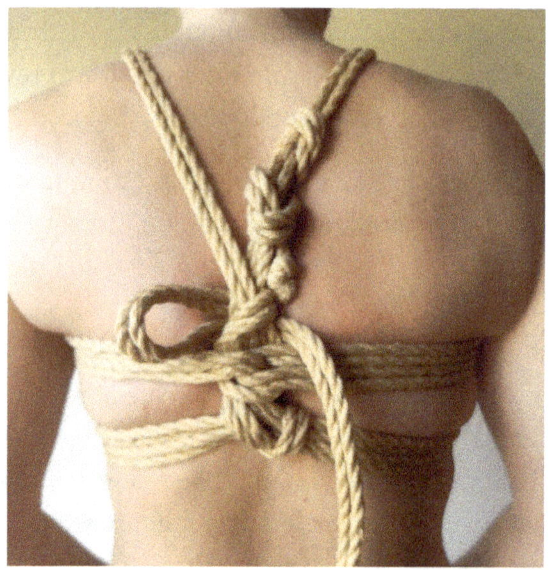

Step 10: Pull the working end of the rope to the right side of the "V-shaped shoulder straps."

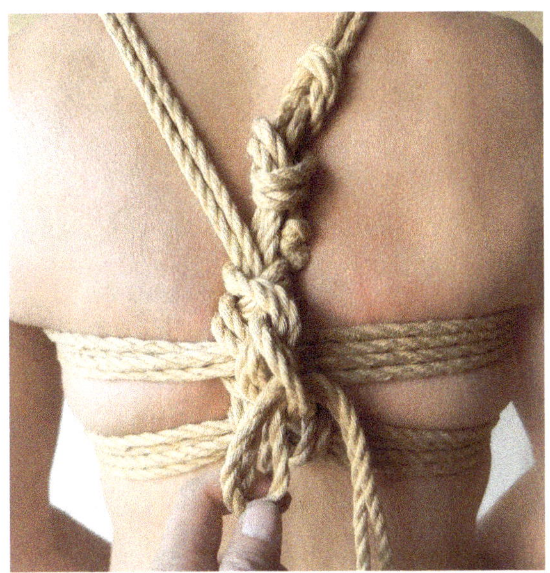

Step 11: Create a small bight with the working end right next to the base of the shoulder straps. Thread the bight through the loop you created in Step 10. For a tighter chain, pull on the working end to make the link smaller.

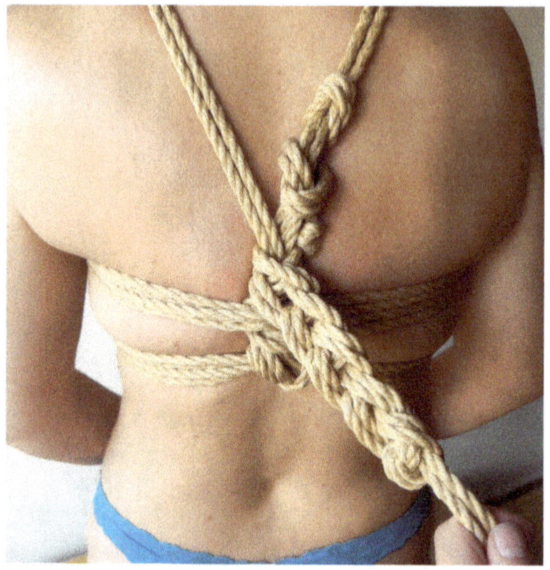

Step 12: Keep repeating Step 11 until you run out of rope. On the last link, pull the working end through the loop completely.

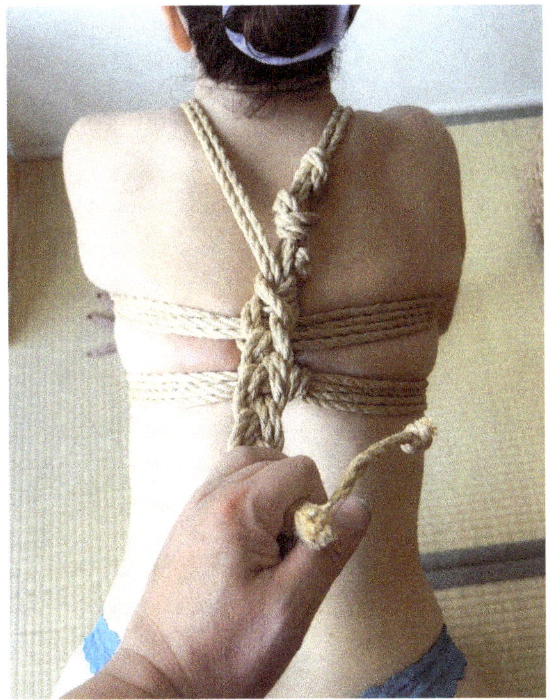

You are all done - now you have a short leash you can use to control your partner.

Option B - Hands Behind Her Back

If the leash doesn't strike your fancy, there are always other options. After all, free hands could be a nuisance, and you might want to restrict her arm movements.

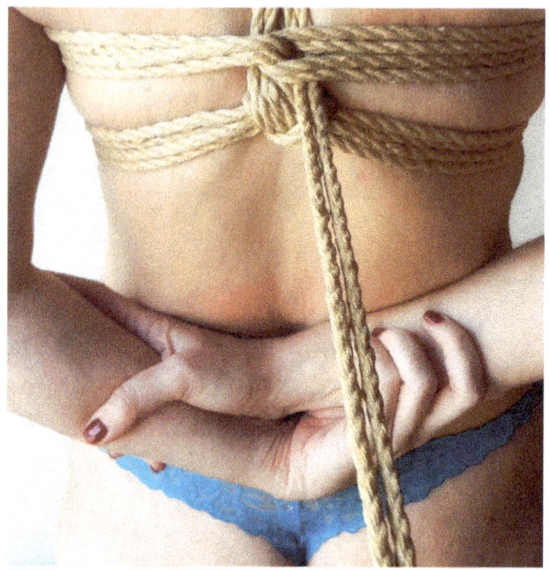

Step 13: Bring the working end straight down past the wrists.

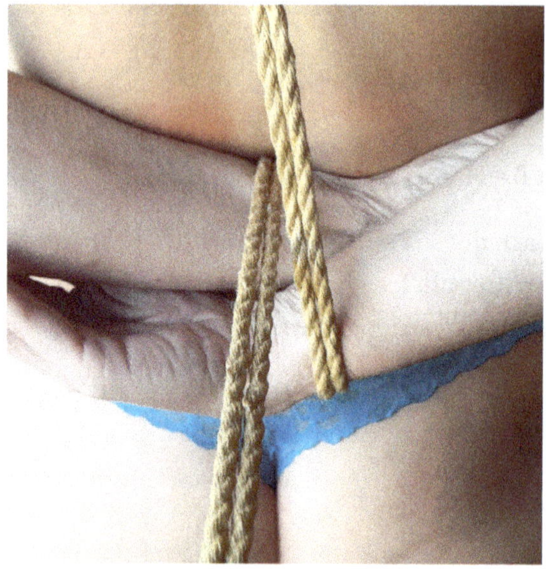

Step 14: Create a single column tie around the wrists by wrapping the rope twice around them.

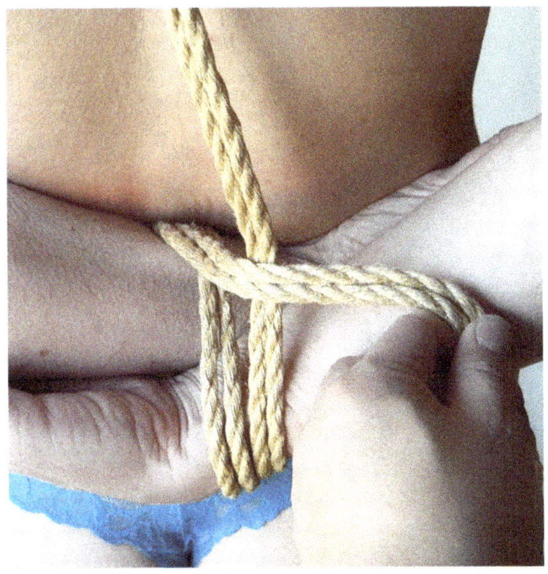

Step 15: Bring the working end across the two parallel bands you have formed.

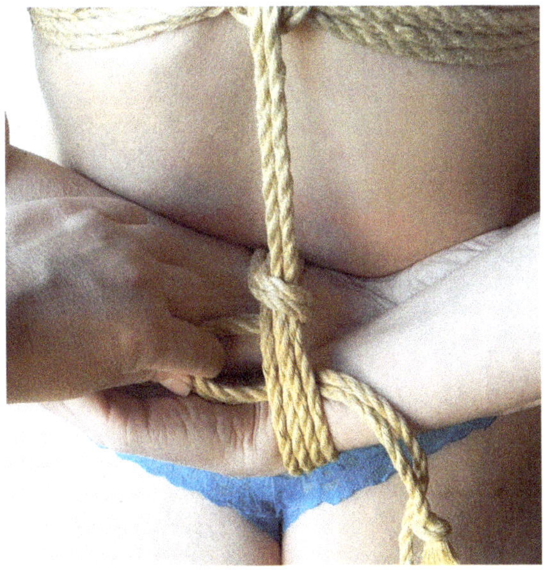

Step 16: Tuck it under between the rope and the wrists.

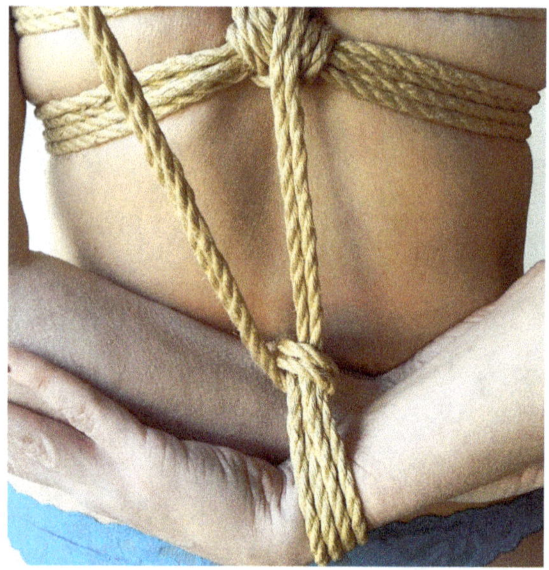

Step 17: Pull the working end through completely.

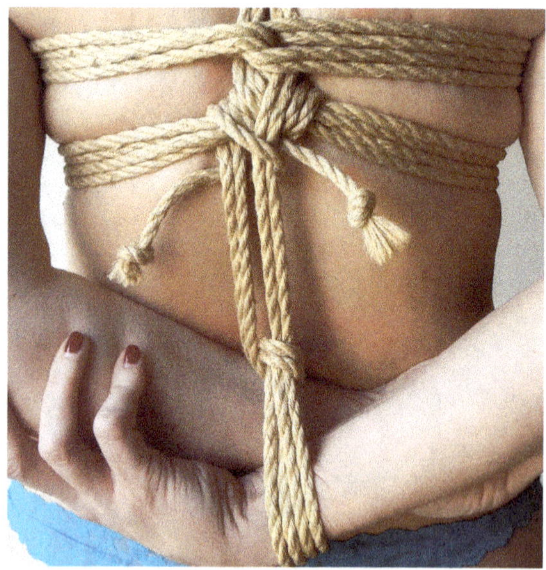

Step 18: Tuck the working end under the bottom horizontal band of the rope so you can tie the rope off.

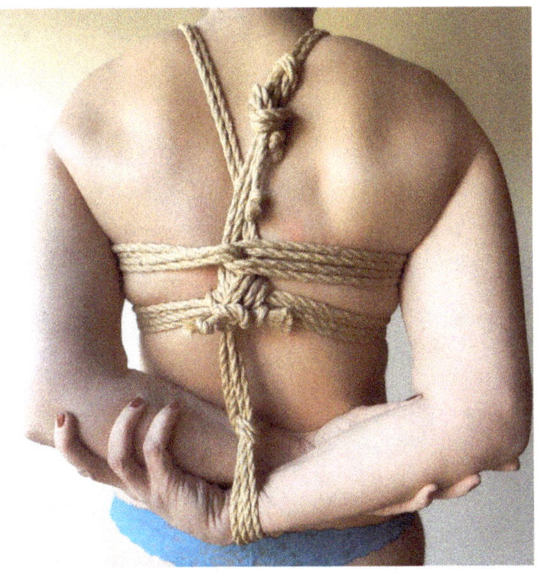

Here is the finished tie combining a chest harness with a single column tie around the wrists.

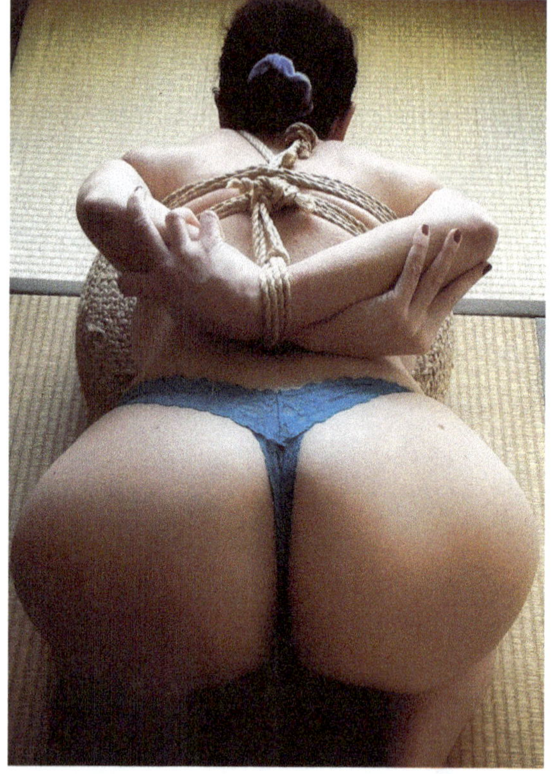

Now you have restricted her arm movements while allowing her mind to wonder. What you do next is entirely up to you....

I want to remind you that the two options presented above are merely that - options; there are endless possibilities you might want to try. My aim in introducing these options is to showcase the "boundless" potential that bondage offers you and your partner (being cheeky since boundless doesn't really apply to your partner here). Think of them as the appetizers; the buffet of bondage fun is all yours to explore. My goal is to tickle your fancy, not burden you with a complicated manual. So, buckle up, improvise, explore, and take your partner on a rollercoaster ride of excitement!

Below are some photos illustrating variations of the same concept we just practiced in Option B - a chest harness with arms bound using nylon rope - to highlight the possibilities.

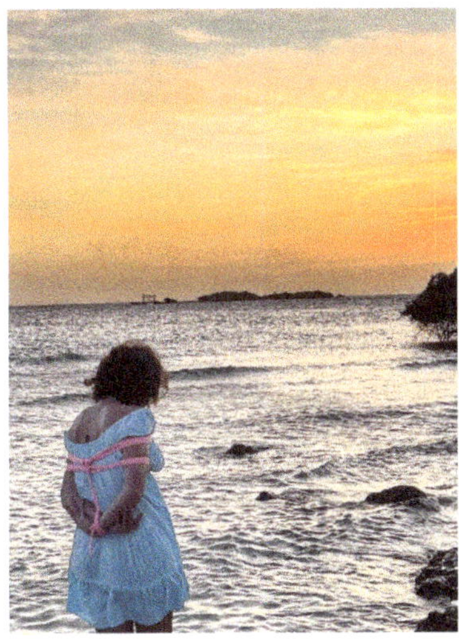

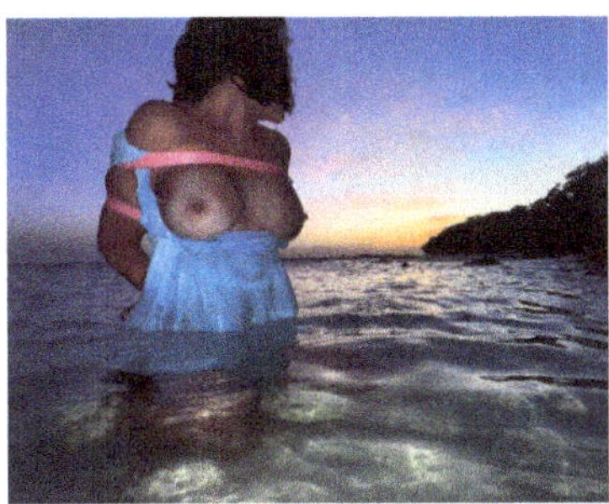

2

CHEST HARNESS VARIATION

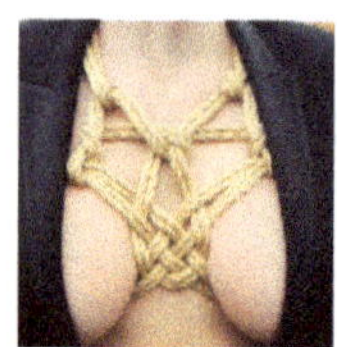

One of the beauties of Shibari is that it offers a beautiful opportunity for boundless creativity. The chest harness variation in this chapter is a product of our freestyle exploration. We hope it serves as an inspiration for you and your partner, igniting your creative sparks to craft something uniquely enjoyable and visually distinctive.

In this version, we crisscross the bands of rope in the middle of the chest.

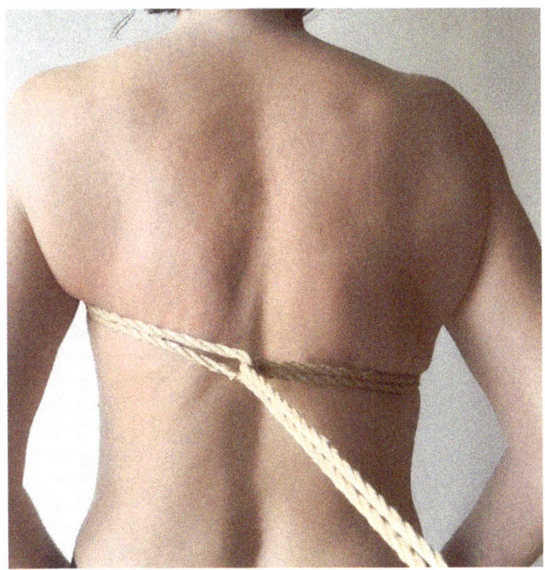

Step 1: Form a lark's head in the middle of the back.

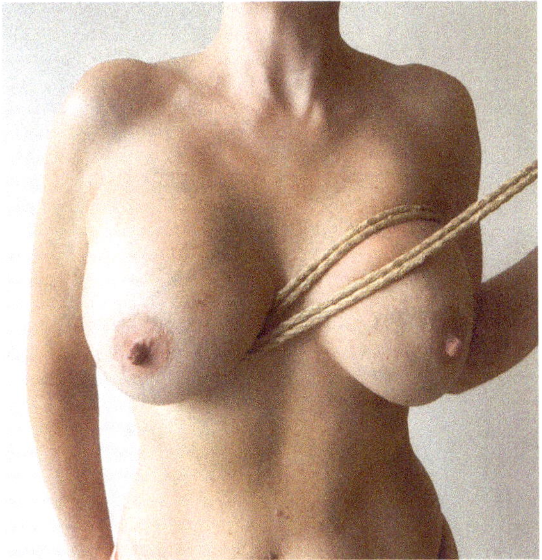

Step 2: Wrap the rope in the opposite direction to create two bands going up diagonally from under the right breast and over the left breast.

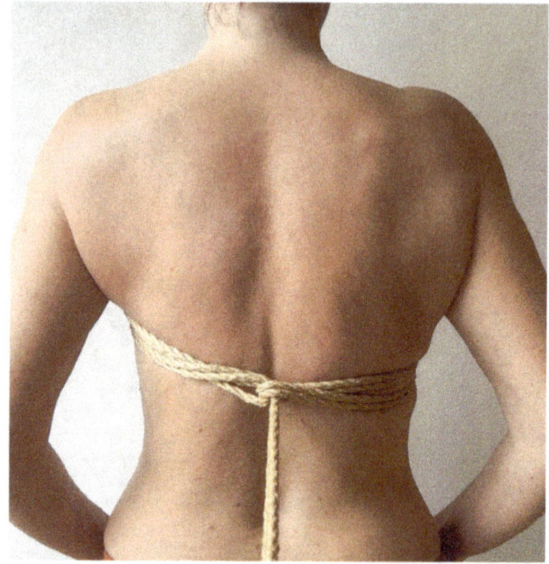

Step 3: Thread the rope through an existing loop (it doesn't matter which loop you thread through)

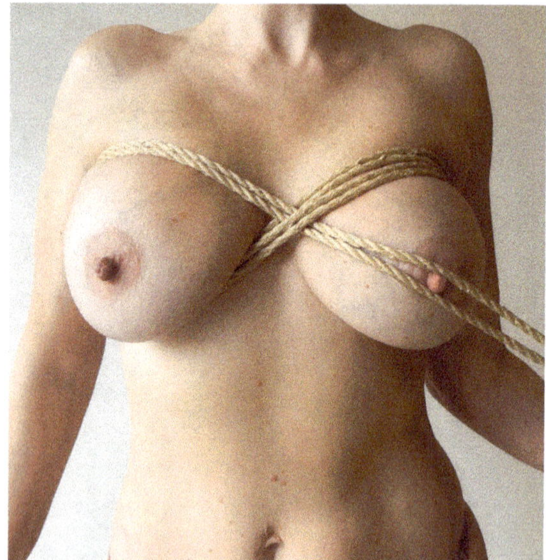

Step 4: Bring the rope back to the front. Thread the rope through the bottom rope. This adds friction between ropes, makes the bands stay together better, and adds visual complexity.

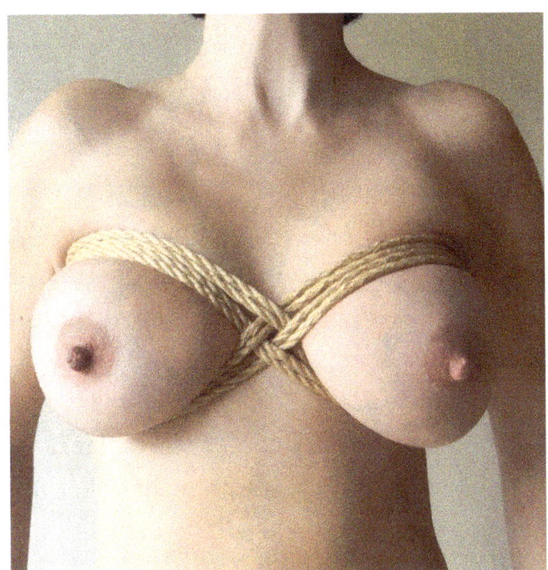

Step 5: Alternate the pattern by threading the working end under the "top" band.

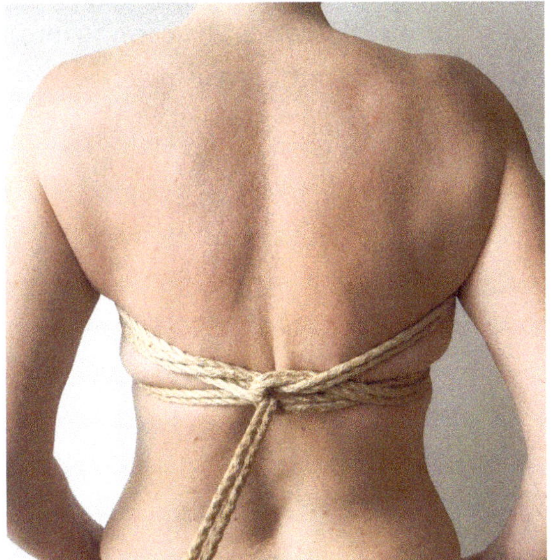

Step 6: Thread the working end of the rope through one of the loops.

At this stage, you've successfully crafted a simple yet elegant chest harness and can go ahead and tie off the remaining rope to ensure the chest harness remains firmly in place.

A Note on Intimacy: If you prefer a more assertive approach (enjoy manhandling your partner) and are interested in using this chest harness for added control during intimate moments (ride her from behind), you will need to make the harness a little tighter. This is particularly important because this style of harness lacks any rope support over the shoulders, which means that if you pull on it while in a rear-facing (doggie style) position, there's a risk of it slipping down.

If you're feeling ambitious, you have the option to extend your rope and continue this tie along with me, creating something a bit more intricate. Before you proceed, it's always wise to lock in your current tie to prevent it from coming loose.

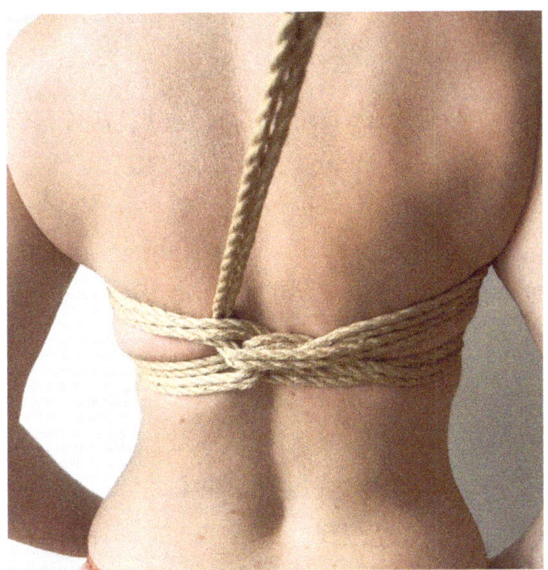

Step 7: Thread the working end of the rope under the top band from the bottom on the left.

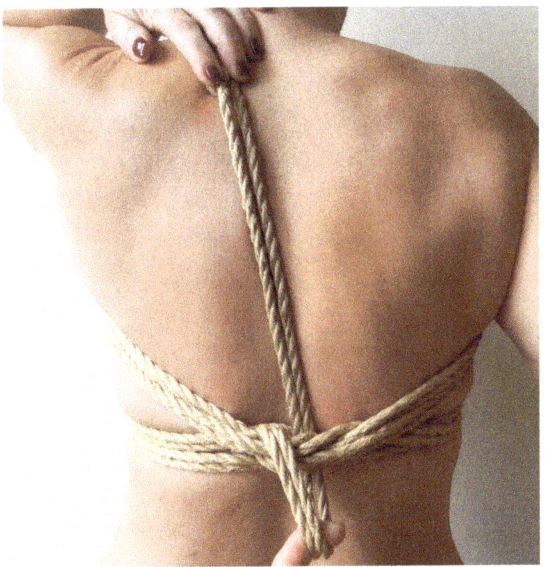

Step 8: Bring the working end down and tuck under the other bands. Pull it out on top on the right.

Rope Extension

If you find yourself in a situation where you're running out of rope and need to extend it, please refer to steps 9-11 for guidance on rope extension using a lark's head knot. Please note that the point at which you may need to extend the rope can vary depending on the length of your rope and the size of your partner.

When extending the rope, you have the flexibility to position the lark's head knot at any point along the rope by reversing the lark's head (to make a reverse lark's head). This offers two key advantages: firstly, it enables you to situate the bulkier knot away from the more sensitive areas of the body; secondly, it allows for improved aesthetics by positioning the knot in a less conspicuous location.

For additional reference, lark's head / reverse lark's head and their use in bondage are covered in greater detail in my first book Knot Tying 101: The Ultimate Beginner's Pocket Guide to 7 Most Useful Knots You Will Ever Need for Shibari.

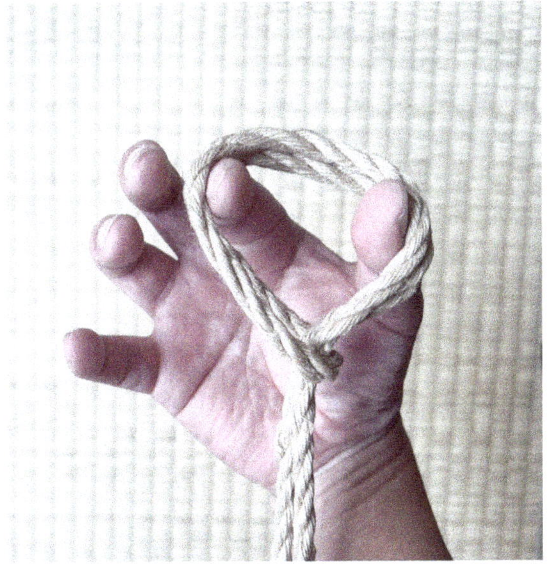

Step 9: Extend the rope to continue the pattern by forming a lark's head on the new rope.

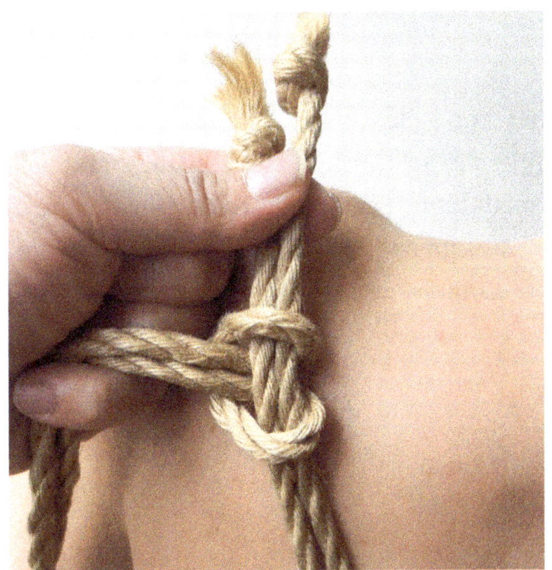

Step 10: Position the lark's head approximately 2-3" from the end of the rope.

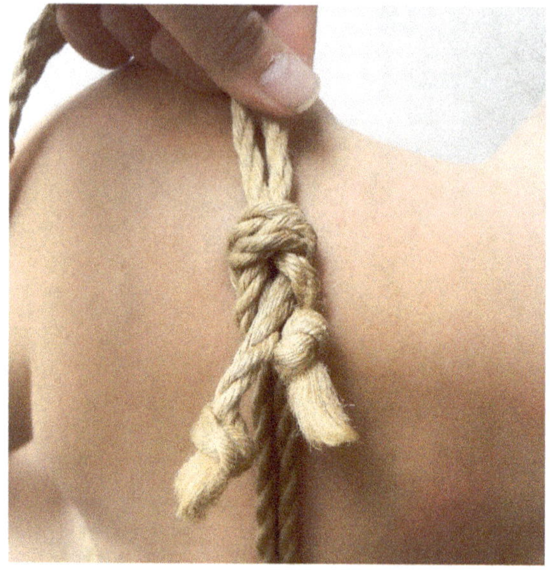

Step 11: Fold the working end to make a reverse lark's head. Pull the rope to tighten the knot.

Now that rope has been extended, we can continue alternating thread through the existing bands of rope to form a 'medallion.' Feel free to follow the next few steps to adopt my design suggestion or modify it to create a variation that resonates more with your personal style and preferences.

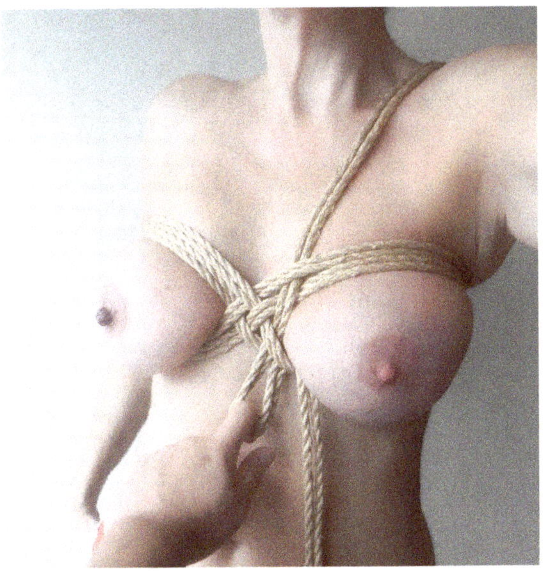

Step 12: Thread the working end under the first band and bring the working end over the top of the second band.

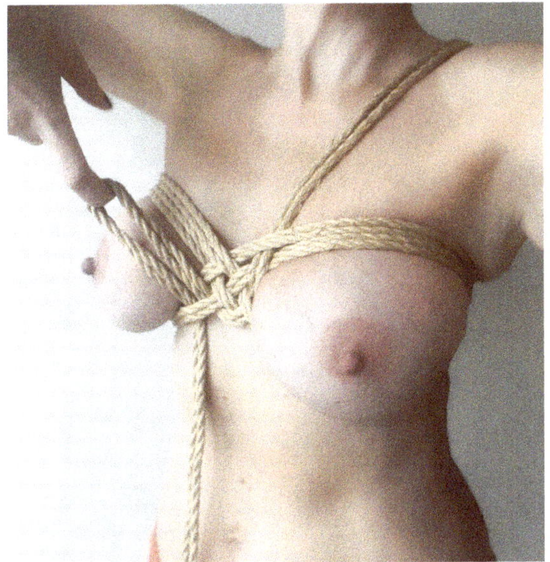

Step 13: Bring the working end of the rope to the right side and thread it under the existing band, as shown.

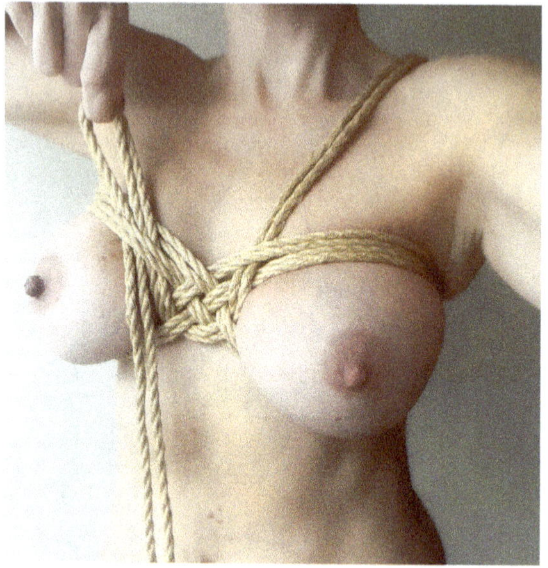

Step 14: Weave the working end through the existing bands of rope as described previously.

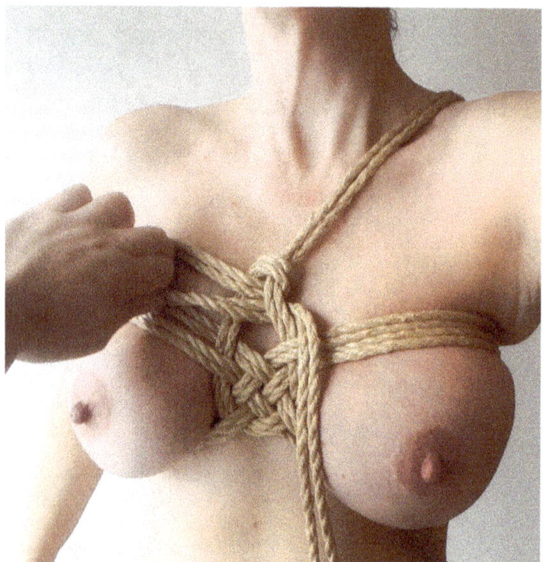

Step 15: Create a half hitch and bring the working end over the right shoulder.

Note: The half hitch added in Step 15 is entirely optional and added here primarily for aesthetics purposes. Alternatively, you can pull the working end straight up and over the right shoulder, though this approach may result in a visually less compelling, geometrically simpler presentation.

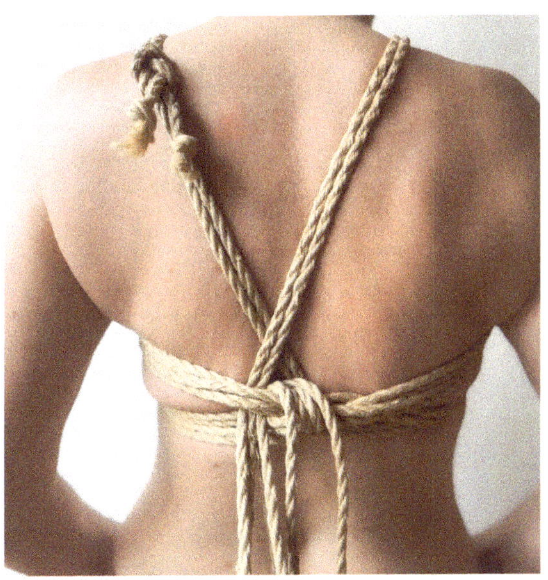

Step 16: Tuck the working end under the top and bottom bands on the left side. (Note: I only showed threading under the first band in this picture.)

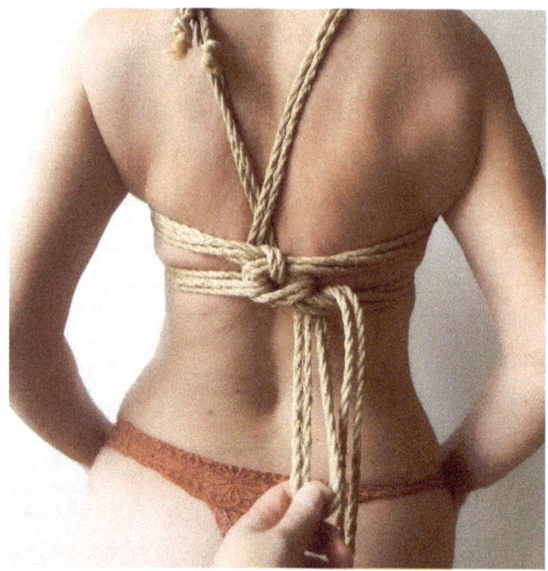

Step 17: Bring the working end to the right side, tuck under the bottom band, and pull through.

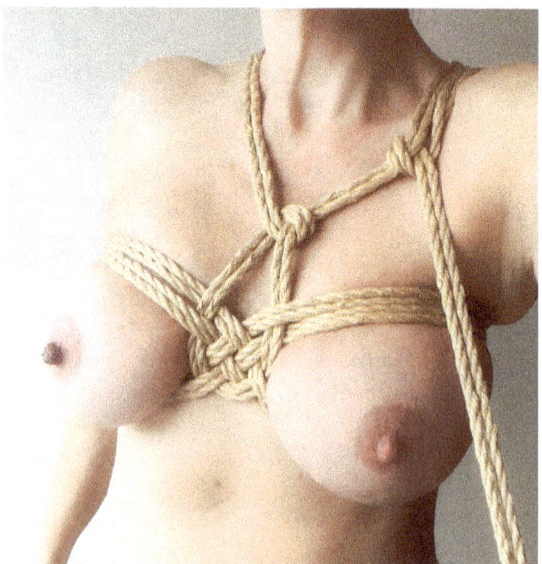

Step 18: Bring the rope back to the front and make a half hitch with the adjacent rope just slightly below the collarbone.

Note: In this case, the addition of the half hitch is to interrupt the look of two parallel bands. Inevitably, some part(s) of a tie will always lose tension during play; this additional half hitch will help maintain the look of the pattern you have designed by helping this outer band stay in place even when it loses tension.

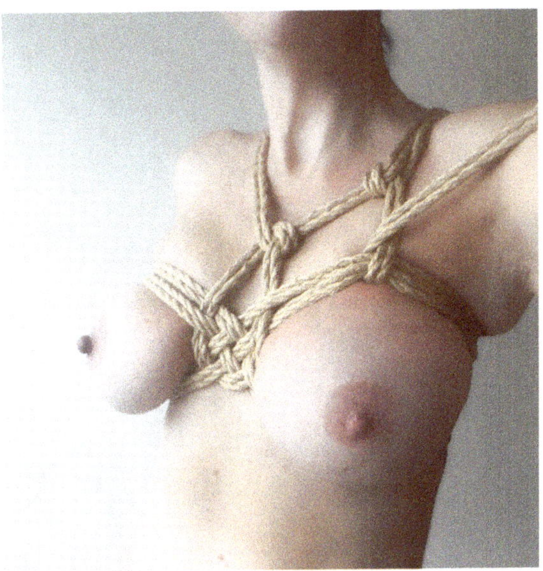

Step 19: Now thread the working end under the band and pull it back up.

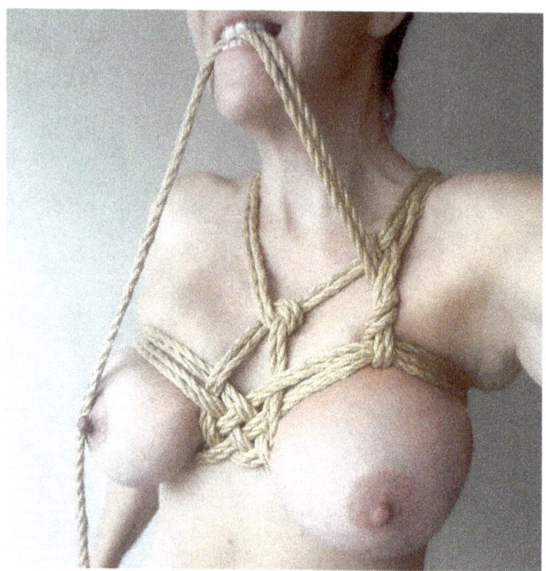

Step 20: Cross the working end and tuck under.
(Pulling the rope with your teeth is optional 😎)

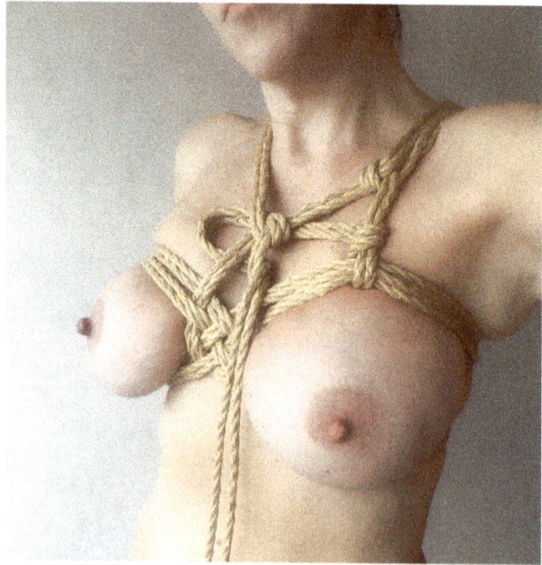

Step 21: Tuck the working end under the half
hitch you created earlier in the middle of the
chest.

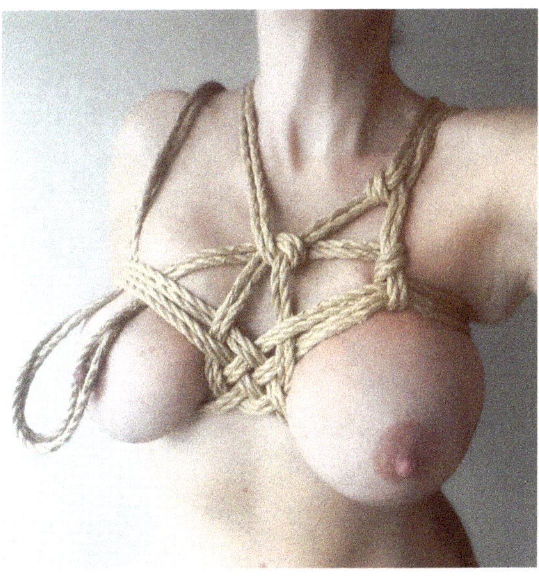

Step 22: Thread the rope under the bands above the right breast and pull it through.

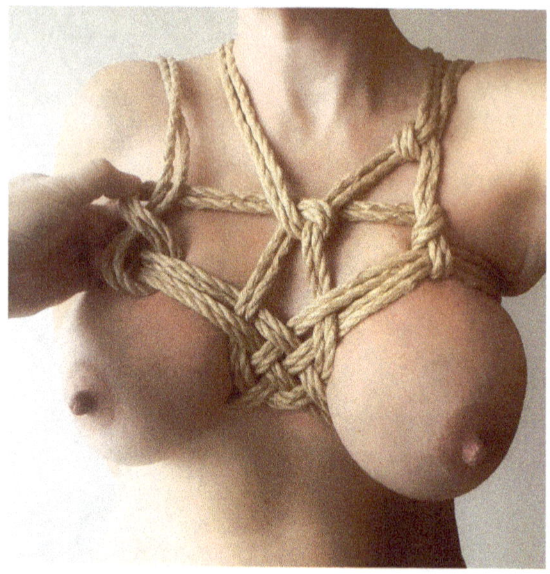

Step 23: Hook the rope from the right side (inside) with one of the left fingers and twist your forearm towards the outside (counterclockwise) to create a small loop. Pull the working end through this loop you have just created.

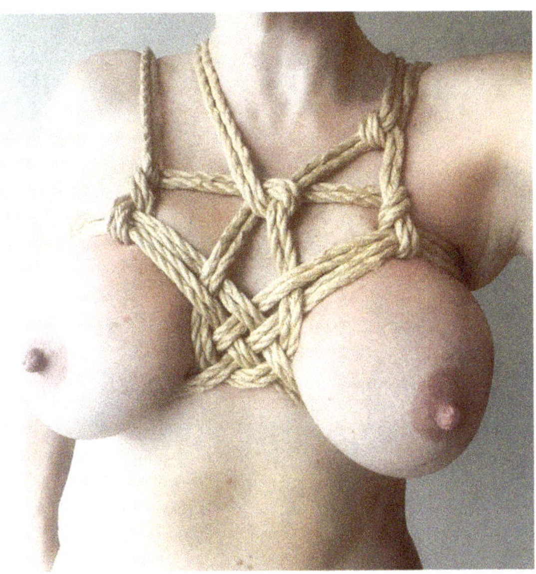

Step 24: Adjust the rope so it is a mirror image of the first (left) side. Repeat what you did on the left side by making a half hitch just below the collarbone before pulling the working end over the right shoulder.

We are almost at the end of this tie. If you have managed to maintain your patience so far, you are doing great. In the upcoming steps, I will demonstrate how to use up the remaining rope by crafting a 'handle' before a final tie-off.

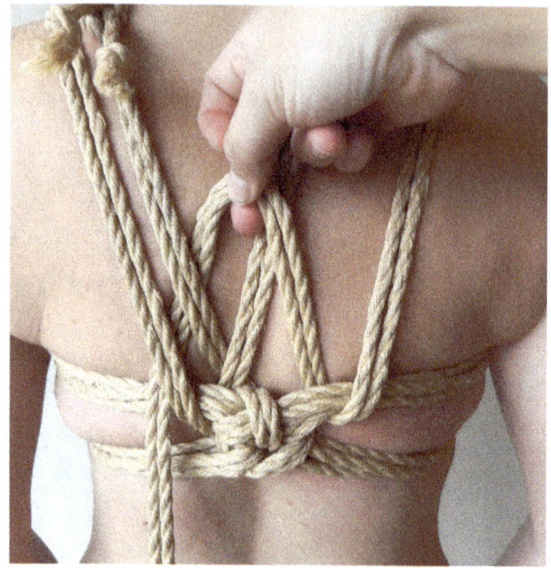

Step 25: Pull the working end under a top band on the right side

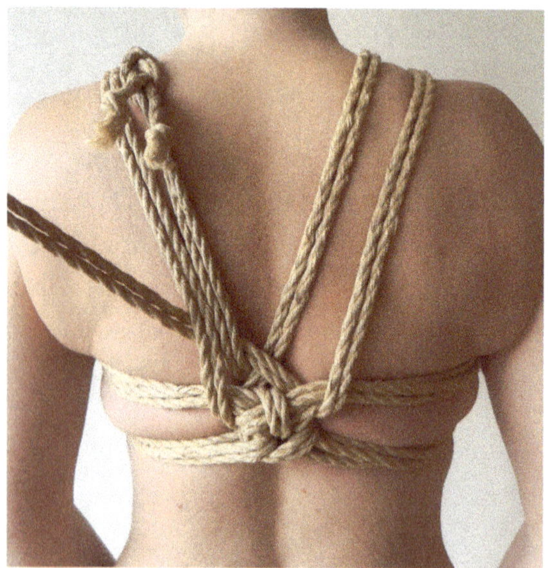

Step 26: Tuck the working end under the two bands of rope on the left side.

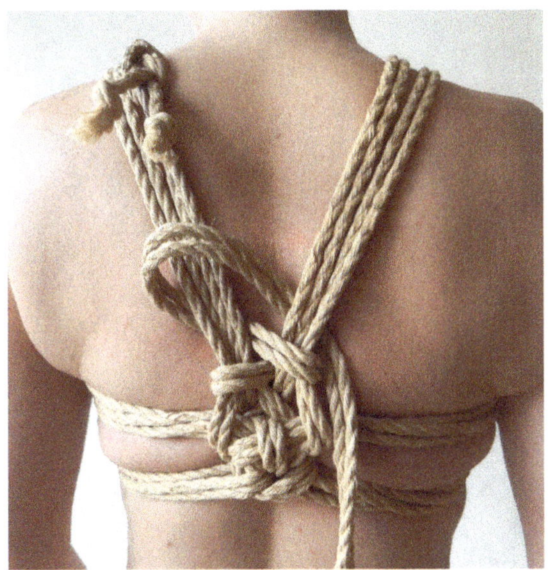

Step 27: Bring the working end back around and tuck under the two bands of rope on the right.

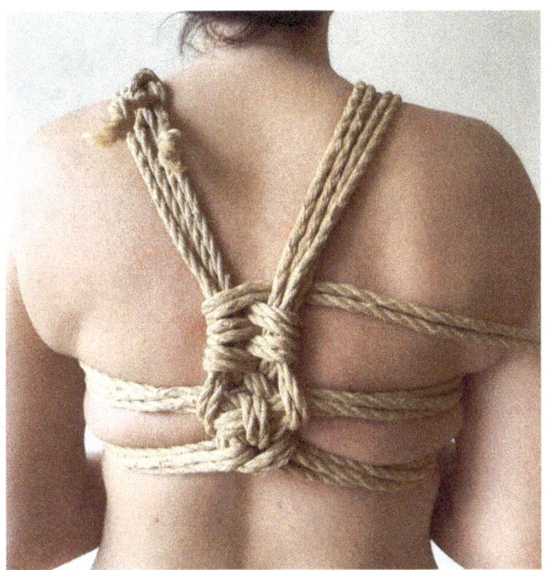

Step 28: Repeat this pattern several times

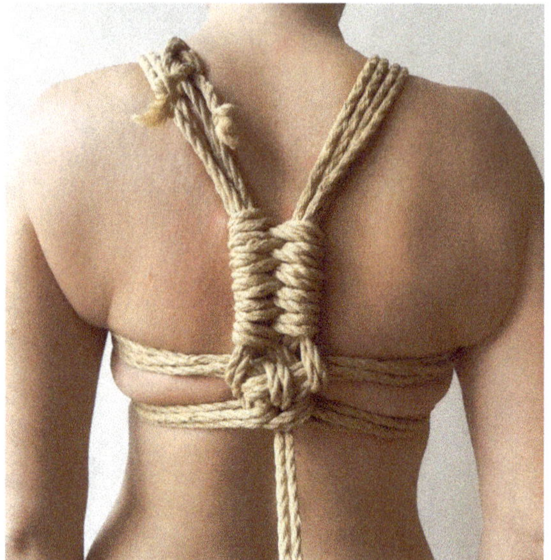

Step 29: Tuck the working end under the pattern you have just created.

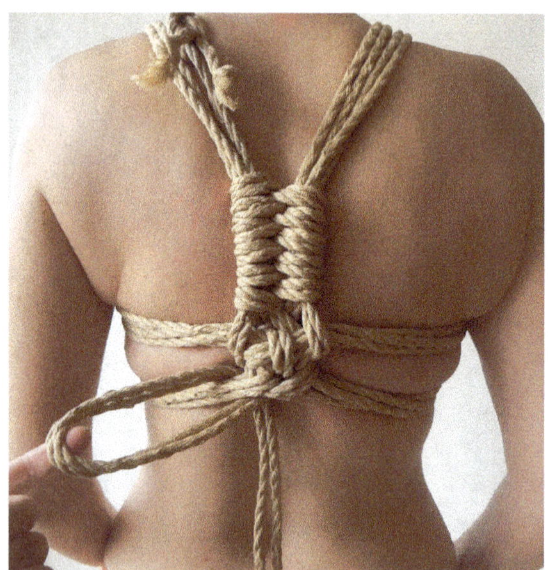

Step 30: Tuck the working end behind the left bottom band and pull through.

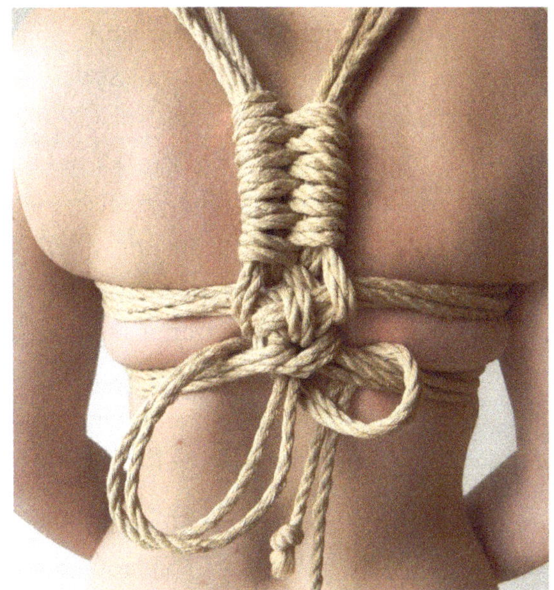

Step 31: Bring the working end around to the right side and tuck it behind the bottom band.

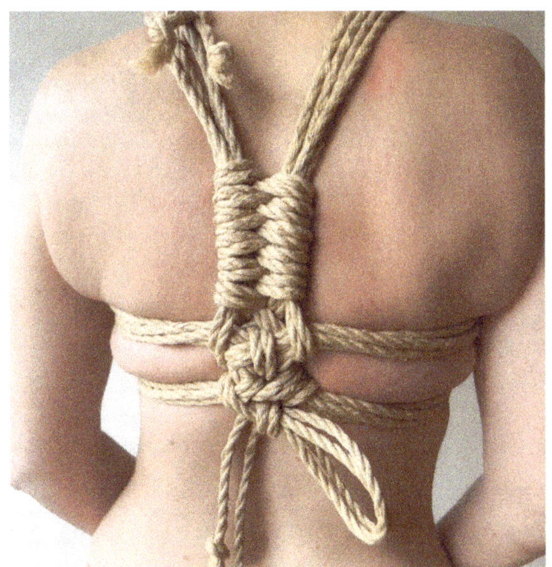

Step 32: Secure the tie. This is how I chose to tie it off.

Because your arms are not bound, you could wear it and go about your everyday business…, and should you and your partner decide to be more adventurous, you can even wear it in public under a low-cut blouse or a light jacket as a fashion statement/accent. In the context of BDSM, wearing a harness could symbolize or imply ownership of the person who is wearing the harness. Your partner may find wearing a harness discreetly under a shirt while out with you exhilarating. This subtle suggestion of your presence could enhance their sense of allure and confidence, whether enjoying a movie or engaging in everyday tasks.

You could pair it with a formal jacket for a more suggestive look (pictured without a bra by my lovely rope bottom)

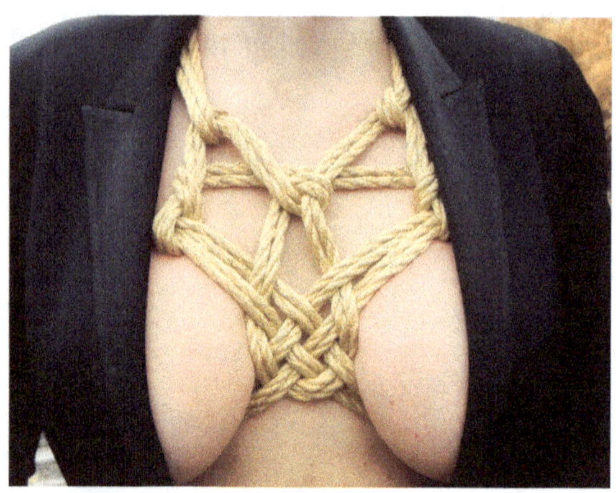

By now, you likely have seen some form of rope bondage in mainstream culture, which can be seen in fashion, photography, and performance art, reflecting a broader cultural fascination with the aesthetics of rope bondage and its overall integration into mainstream culture.

The ensemble captured below is only appropriate for the most daring partners and should be reserved for events supporting such a dress code. Yet, the underlying principle is clear: rope is incredibly versatile, suitable for a spectrum of activities that span from binding to liberating or even a combination of both. The choice is entirely yours. I am here to show you the various paths out there; which one you take and how far you go is solely up to you and your partner.

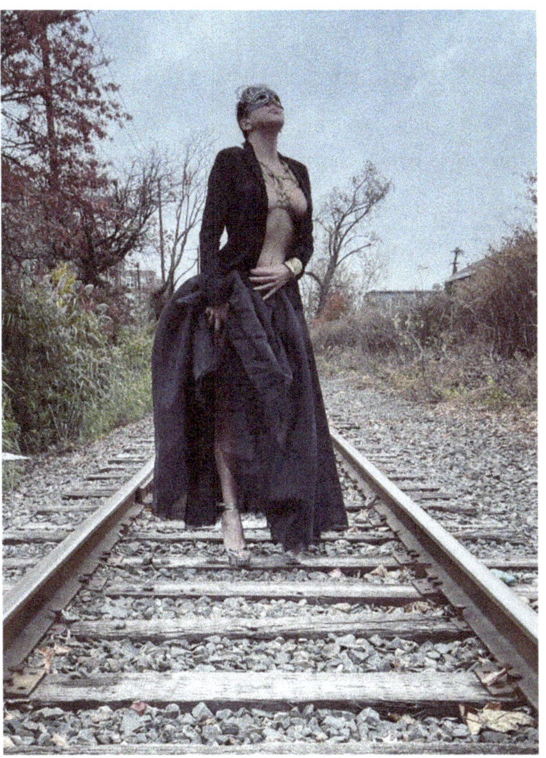

LEAVE A REVIEW

Did this book help you in some way? If so, I'd love to hear about it. Leaving a review isn't just about sharing your thoughts – it's about helping fellow readers find the right book to fit their needs and supporting the author in crafting even more amazing content for the next book!

Go ahead and spread the knot-tying love with a review!

If you got this book from Amazon, you'll find that I've included some additional photos and suggestions at the bottom of the listing to help you get started with practicing these knots immediately. I'm eager to hear about your experience and see photos as part of your review (keep those photos knotty but decent please).

That Rope Guy

3

PENTAGRAM HARNESS

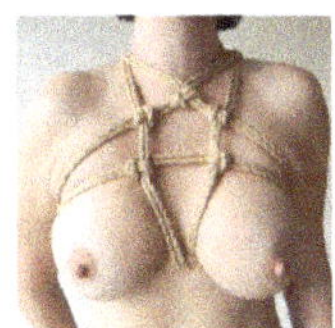

This design involves placing a rope and knot directly over the sternum (breastbone), which may be uncomfortable or undesirable for some individuals. Therefore, obtaining explicit consent from your partner before proceeding with this pattern is crucial.

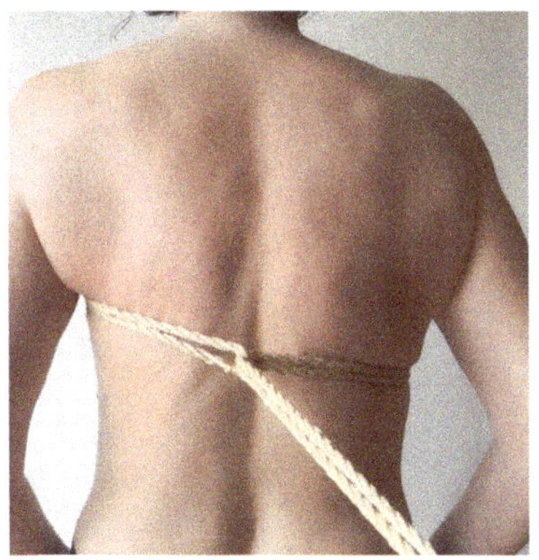

Step 1: Form a lark's head in the middle of the back (note - all chest harnesses presented in this book start the same; a lark's head should come naturally to you by now).

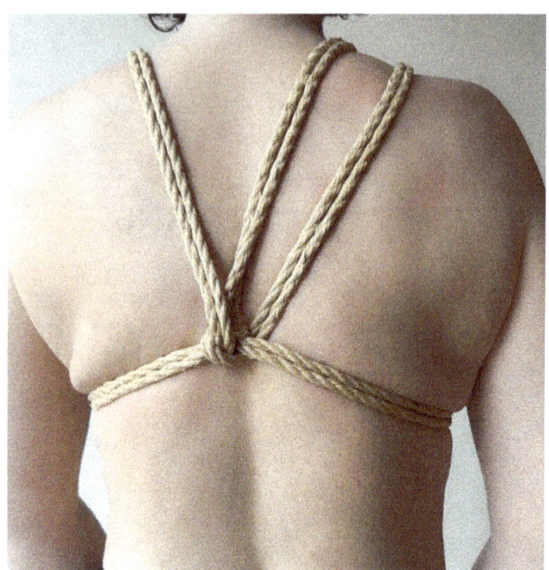

Step 3: Hook the rope around the horizontal rope on the back and bring it around to the front over the right shoulder.

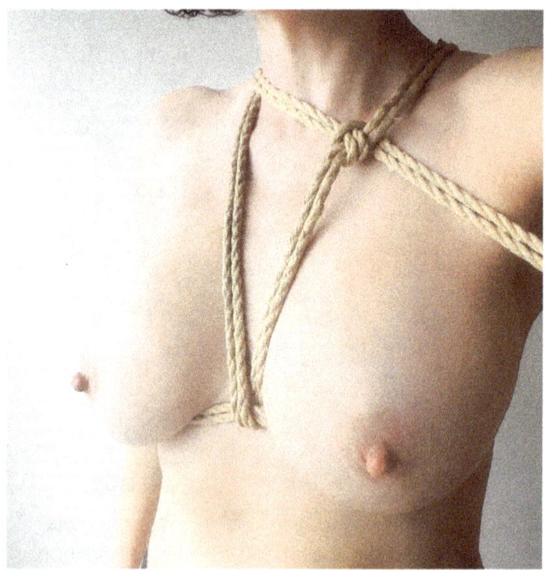

Step 4: Bring the rope across and form a munter's hitch.

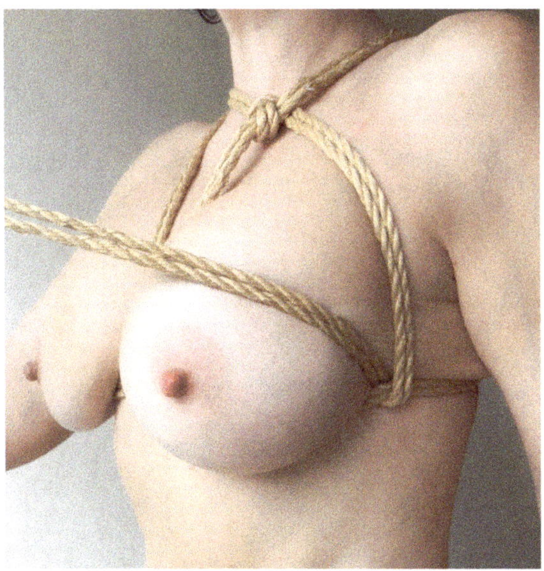

Step 5: Tuck the rope under the horizontal rope next to the left breast.

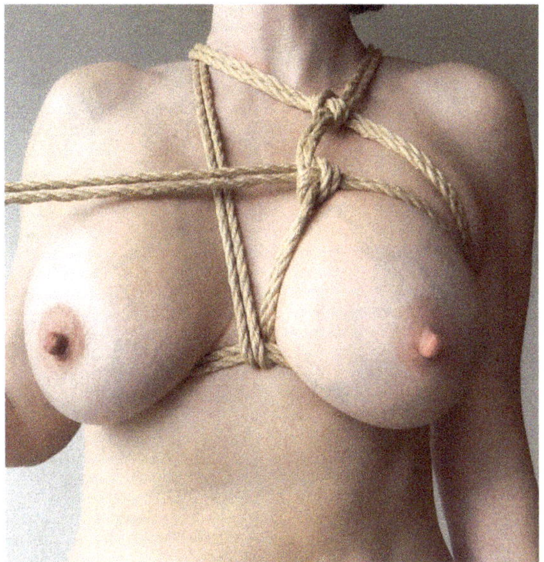

Step 6: Form another munter's hitch over the left breast.

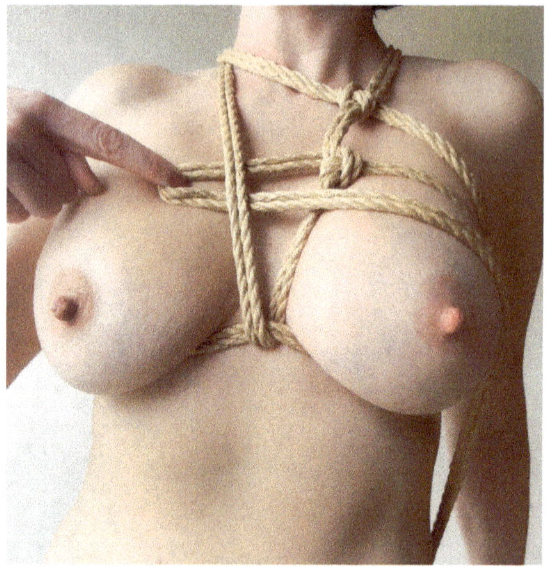

Step 7: Form a reverse munter's hitch by forming a bight under the right shoulder strap,

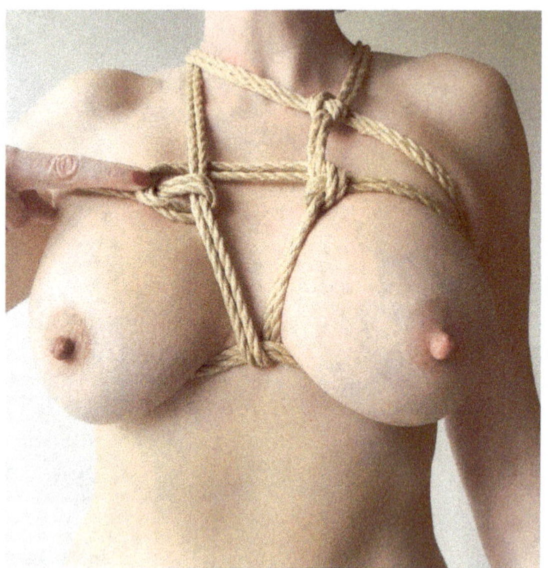

Step 8: Thread the working end through the bight. Adjust the rope to ensure that the munter's hitch is a mirror image of the first one.

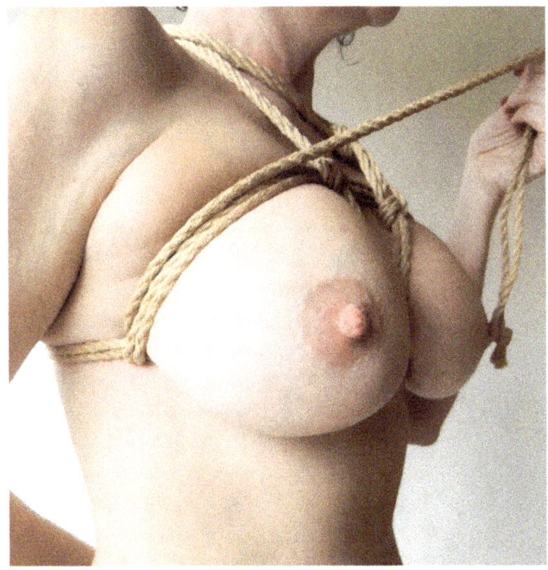

Step 9: Repeat what you did in step 5 by tucking the rope under the horizontal rope next to the right breast.

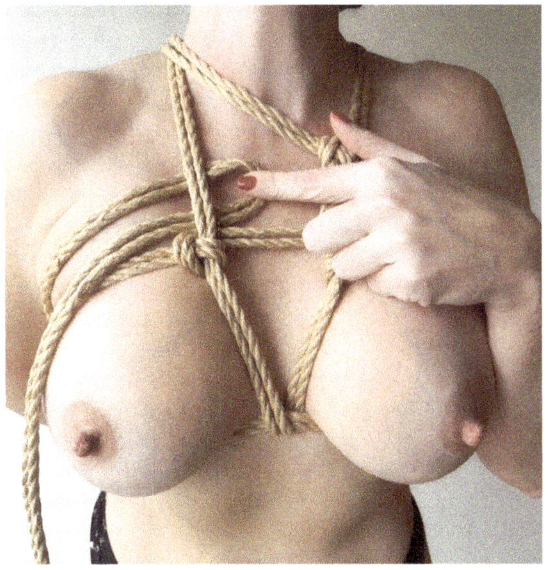

Step 10: Form a reverse munter's hitch following the same instruction in step 8.

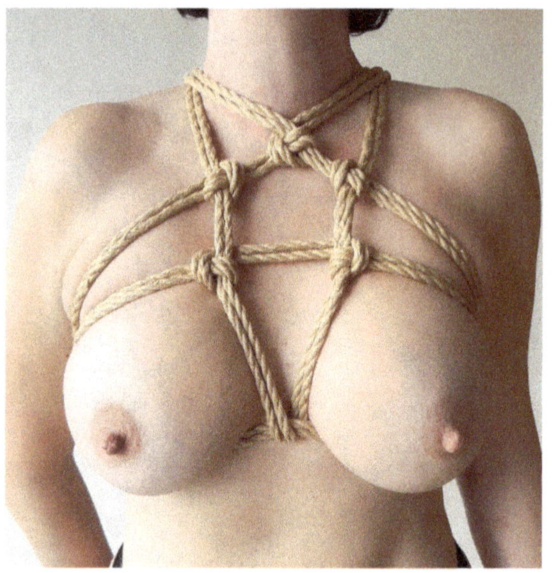

Step 11: Form another munter's hitch between the collarbones at the bottom of the neck.

To secure the harness, bring the rope to the back over the left shoulder and finish the tie (see previous chapters for tie-off examples).

If you appreciate the concept of posture correction through a corset, feel free to continue with a series of modifications to transform the chest harness into a corset/mini dress. If your partner has a significant hip-to-waist ratio, completing the harness at the waist may cause the entire pattern to roll up. Hence, consider extending the design beyond the waist below the hips to ensure a stable and comfortable fit.

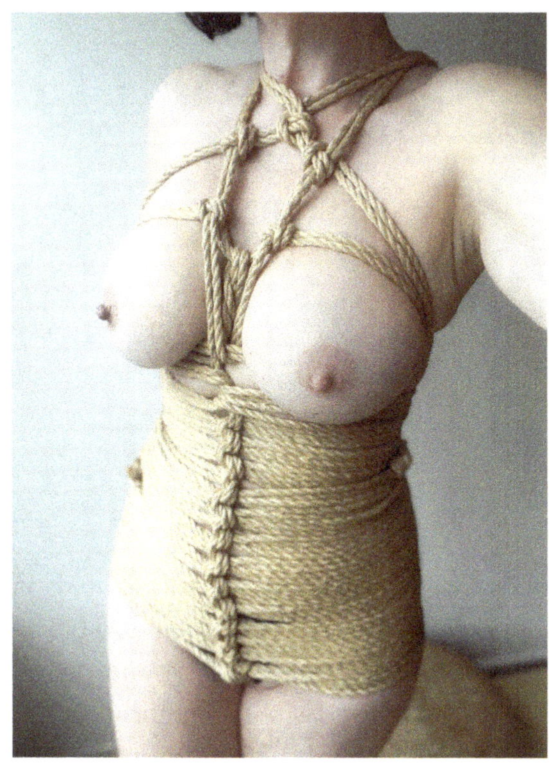

4

LEG BIND

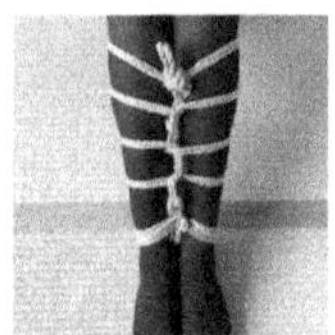

In Shibari, the practice of leg binding holds profound significance, both aesthetically and symbolically. The act of leg binding in Shibari goes beyond mere physical restraint. It represents a deep communication, a dialogue without words, where the rigger (the person doing the tying) and the bottom (the person being tied) engage in a shared experience of vulnerability and control. This dynamic is central to the Shibari experience, where the physical act of binding becomes a medium for emotional and psychological exploration.

Moreover, leg binds in Shibari are not just about the end result but also about the process. The methodical, rhythmic nature of the tying, the sensation of the rope against the skin, and the gradual loss of mobility can be a meditative and deeply sensory experience. For many, it's an exercise in mindfulness and surrender, an opportunity to explore boundaries and trust in a safe, controlled environment.

There is a wide range of leg binding variations, spanning from straightforward to quite intricate and complex designs. The pattern I've chosen to present in this chapter is relatively easy to tie, yet it is a lot of fun to use in the bedroom. This particular style strikes a balance between simplicity and functionality, making it ideal for beginners as well as those looking to add an element of playful restraint in their intimate moments. Furthermore, its versatility allows for creative adaptations, encouraging couples to explore and personalize their Shibari experience.

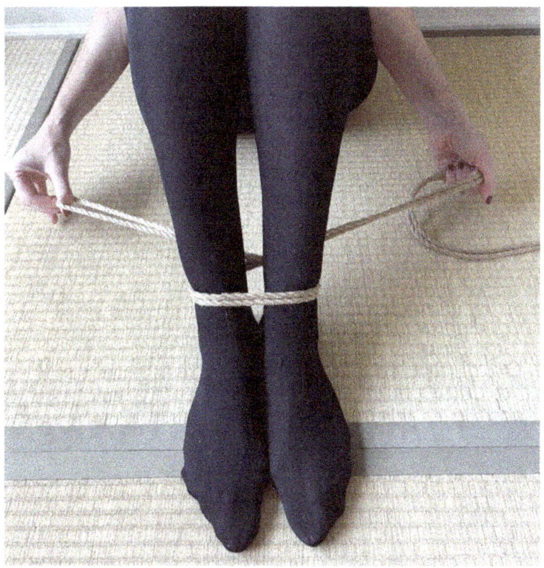

Step 1: Start with a double column tie by wrapping the rope around the ankles. Make sure the bight is about 10 inches for the next two steps.

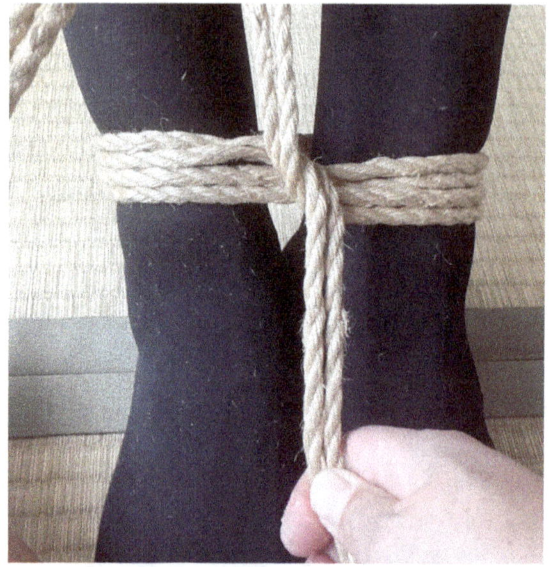

Step 2: Cross the working end and the bight between the two ankles.

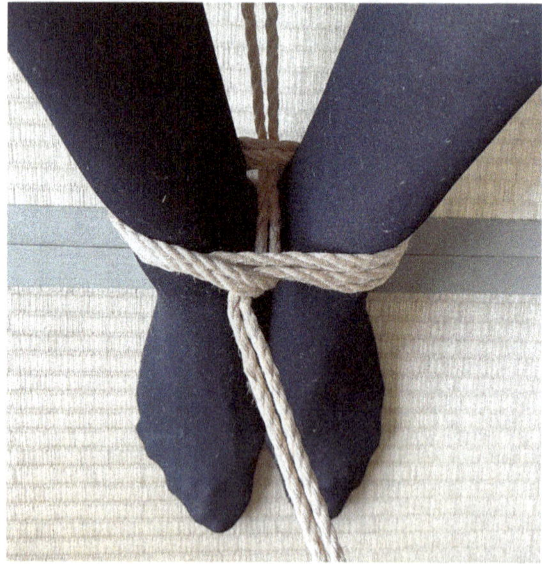

Step 3: Bring the working end around the back and then thread it back out to the front of the ankles.

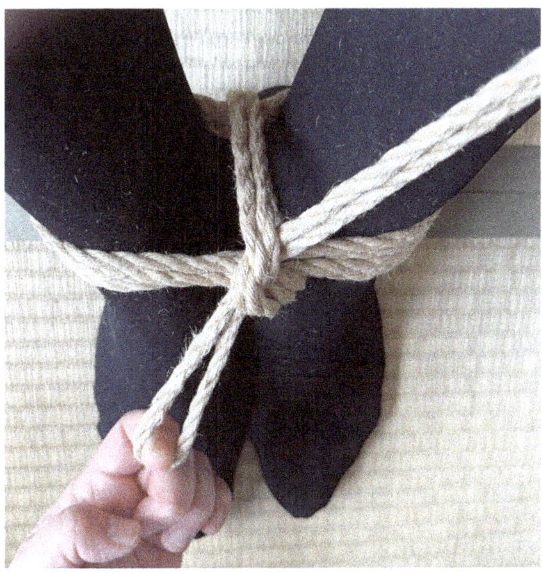

Step 4: Tie a half hitch

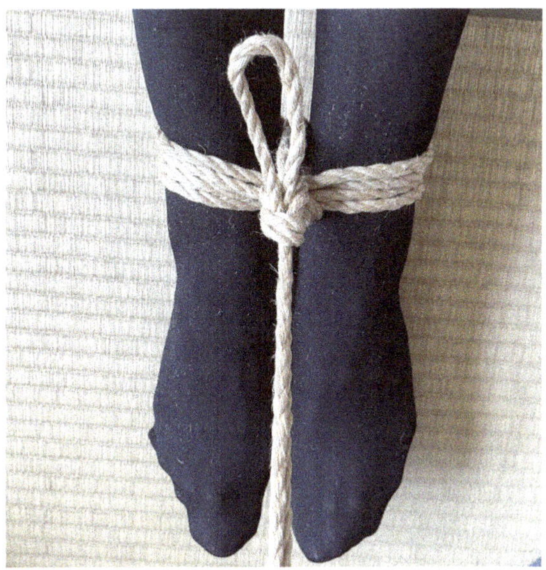

Step 5: Create a square knot in the middle of the double column tie.

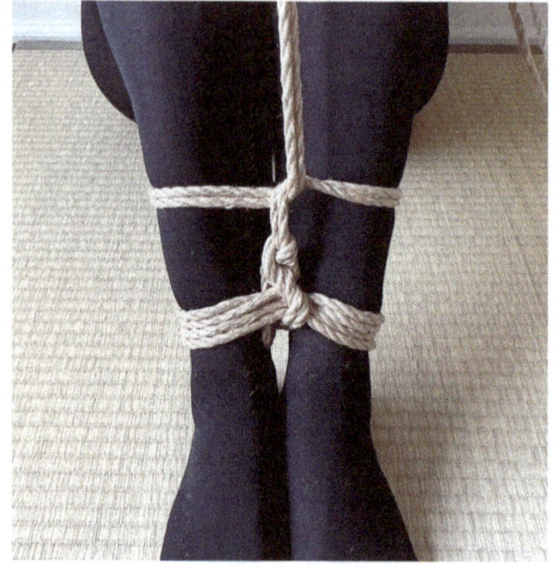

Step 6: Wrap the working end around the calves. Thread the working end under the wrap and pull up.

Note: you can go either right or left for your first wrap in step 6. For me, it really does not matter. In the example illustrated here, I chose to go right to create the first loop around the ankles. Remember the direction you chose in step 6 and reverse direction for each sequential wrap.

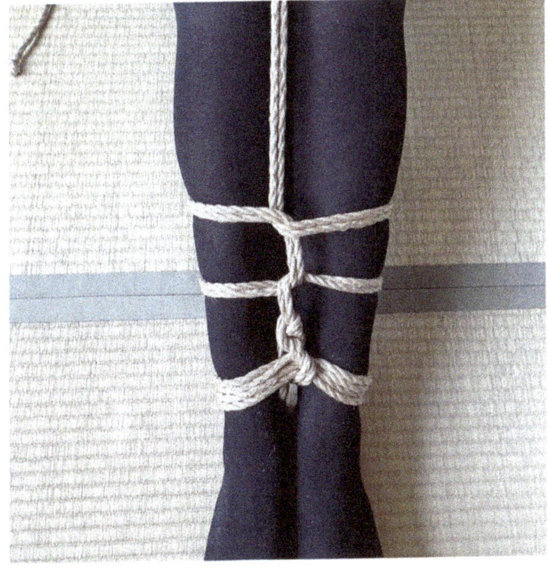

Step 7: Repeat step 6 a few more times.

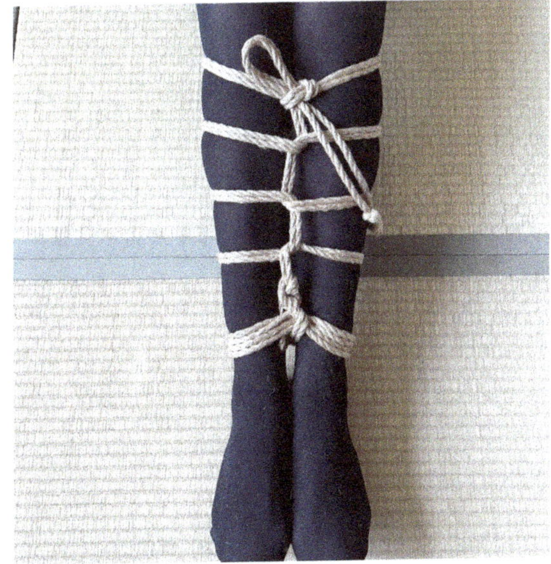

Step 8: Finish the tie just below the back of the knees. (The back of the knee is a vulnerable area, so avoid putting rope in that area.)

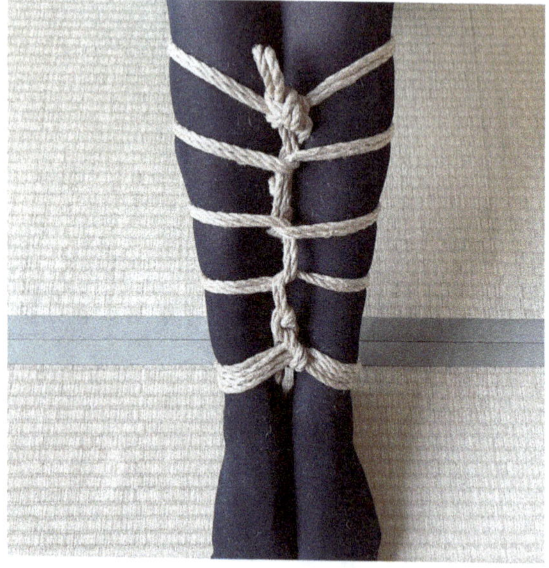

Step 9: Tie off the rope with a square note at the front of the tie.

At this point, you have completed a basic leg bind, but you can repeat the same steps so the pattern continues all the way up to the top of the thighs and then tie-off around the waist.

Improvise

If you have spare rope and wish to restrain your partner's hands, consider exploring this option. There are various options available, and this happened to be something we came upon this occasion.

If your partner doesn't feel at ease with her hands positioned behind her thighs, feel free to opt for an alternative hand placement. Pay close attention to her reaction as you explore more strenuous poses, maintain open communication, and, most importantly, have fun.

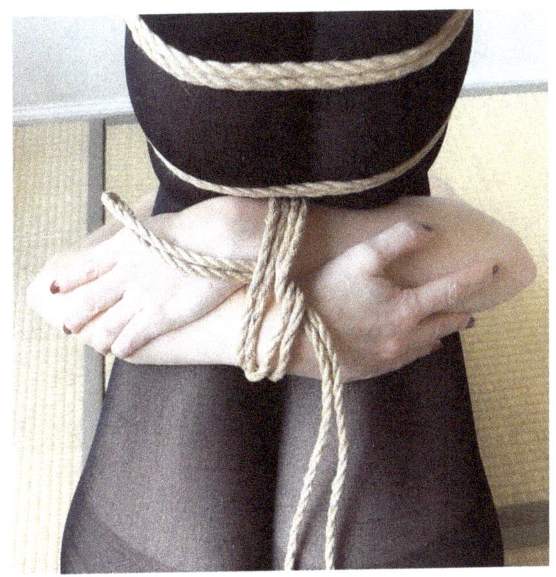

Step 10: Complete a single column tie around the wrists.

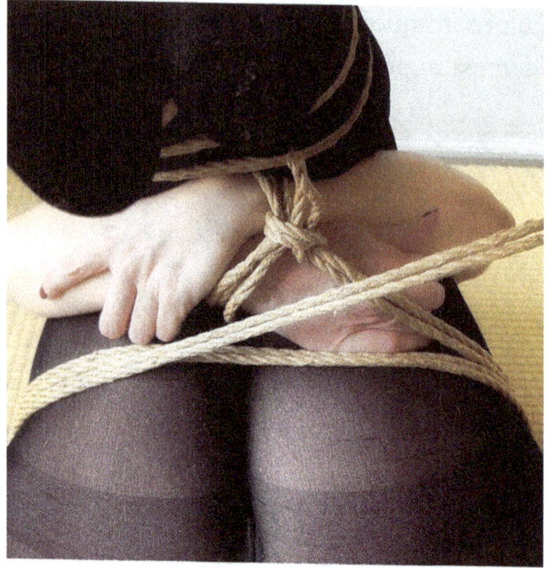

Step 11: Take the working end and wrap twice around the waist and thighs.

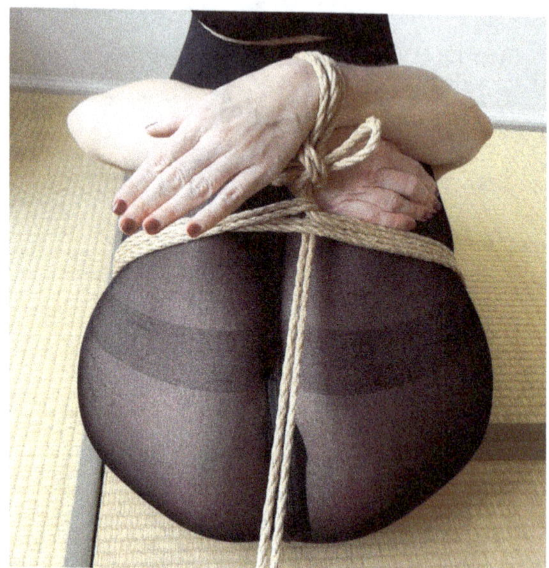

Step 12: Take the working end and tuck it under the two bands of rope you have just created.

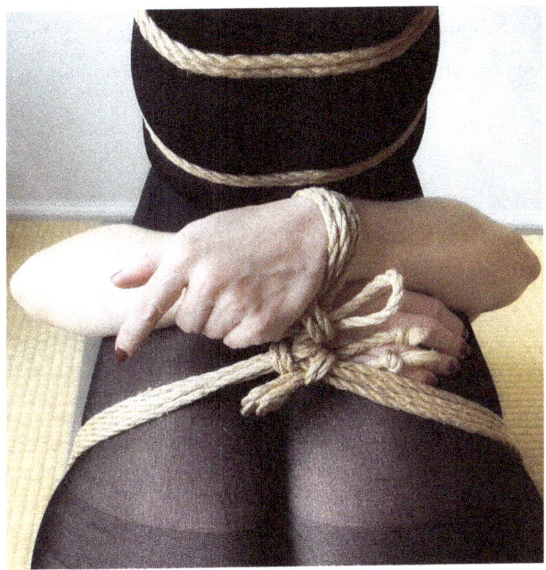

Step 13: Tie off the end of the rope (in this case, I did it with a square knot)

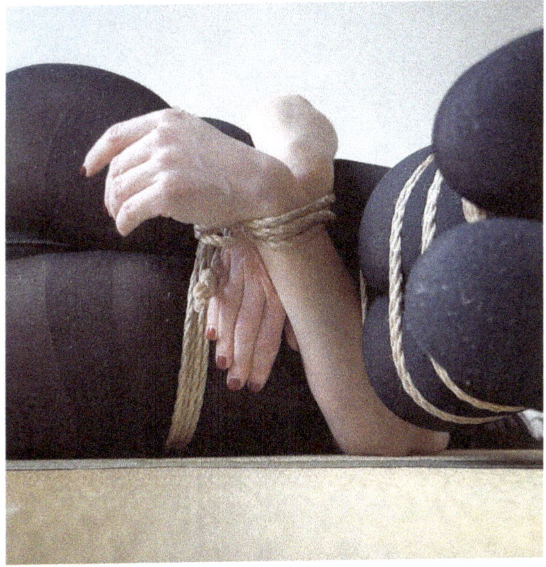

You are now all done!

Included below is a slightly different variation of the full-length leg bind (mermaid tail) using a single nylon rope.

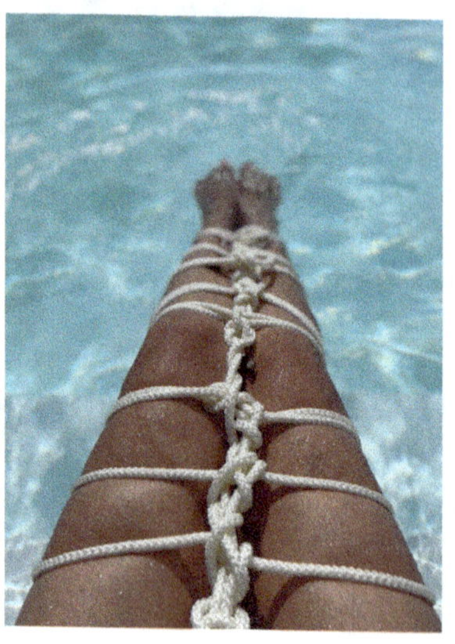

5

FUTOMOMO

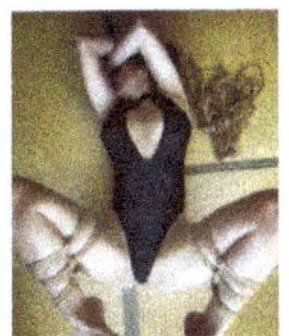

The Futomomo, translating to 'thigh' in Japanese, is a tie that binds the leg in a folded position, creating both aesthetic appeal and immobilization. This tie gained popularity for its striking visual impact and the intense sensations it can produce. In the context of Shibari, the Futomomo tie became more than just a method of restraint; it turned into an intimate form of artistic expression, a way of exploring vulnerability and connection between two individuals.

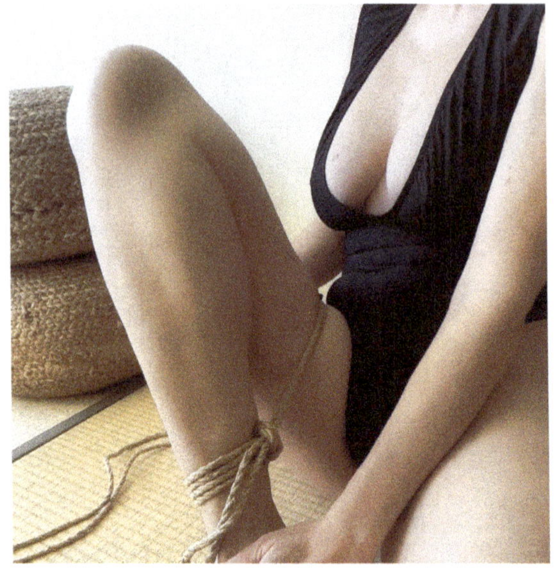

Step 1: Tie a single column tie above the ankle.

As you continue following technical instructions to complete the tie, please remember that as the wraps pass over the shin, which lacks muscles, this tie can be quite painful for the person being tied. Unfortunately, you want to tie this tie a little tighter because as time goes on, the hamstrings tend to loosen, allowing for more leg bending and resulting in loss of tension. Shin pain can be extremely challenging for many people, so maintaining clear communication with your partner is crucial. Sometimes, adjusting the rope by just a fraction of an inch in either direction can significantly alleviate shin pain.

For optimal positioning of these wraps, I recommend placing them as high up on the thigh as feasible while ensuring that the rope does not rest directly in the groin crease.

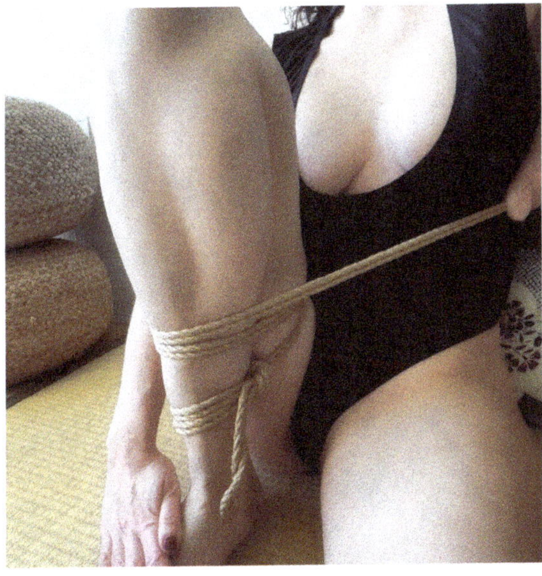

Step 2: Take the working end of the rope and wrap it twice around the thigh/calf.

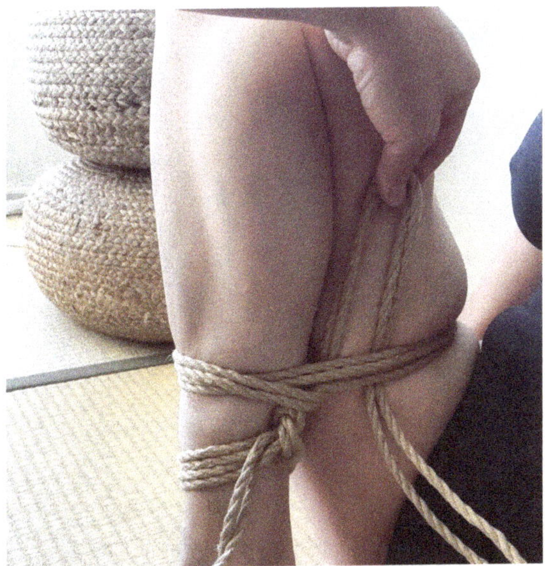

Step 3: Tuck the working end under both wraps and pull up from behind.

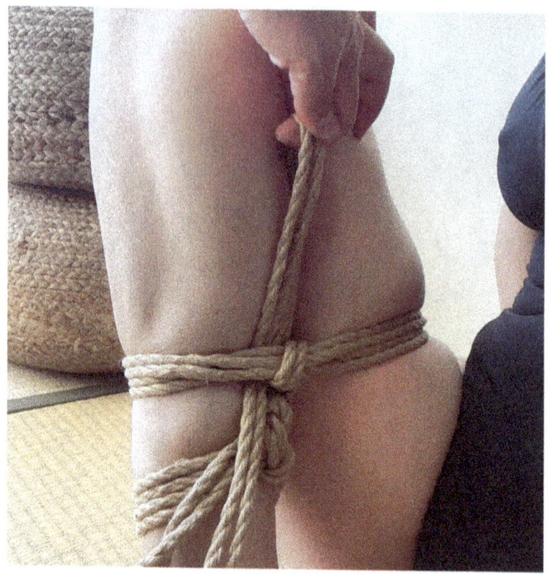

Step 4: Tuck the working end under the entire band of rope and pull up from behind.

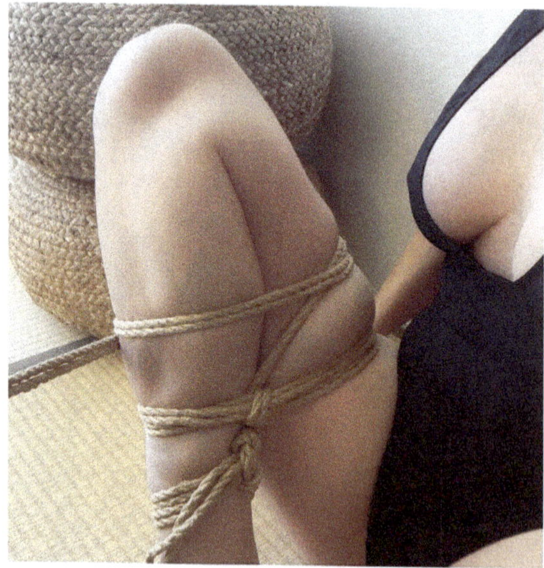

Step 5: Continue your wrap toward the knee.

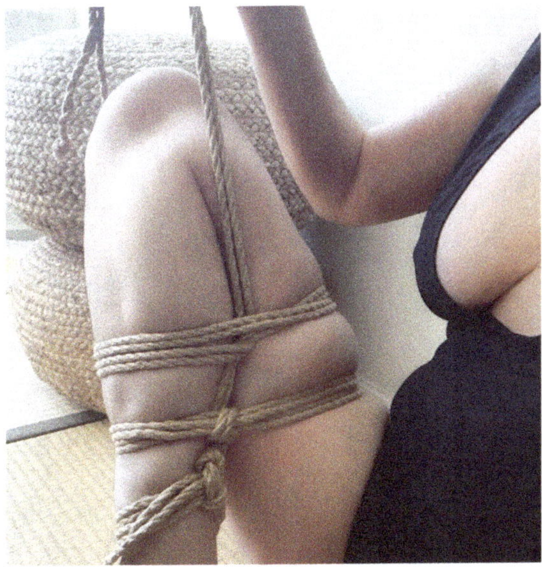

Step 6: Repeat Step 3 by tucking the working end under and pulling through.

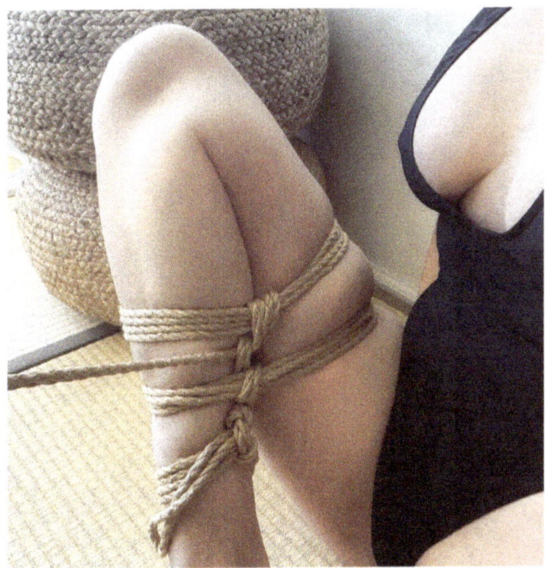

Step 7: Pull down the rope and thread it through between the calf and stem, as shown. (You can also thread the rope through from left to right)

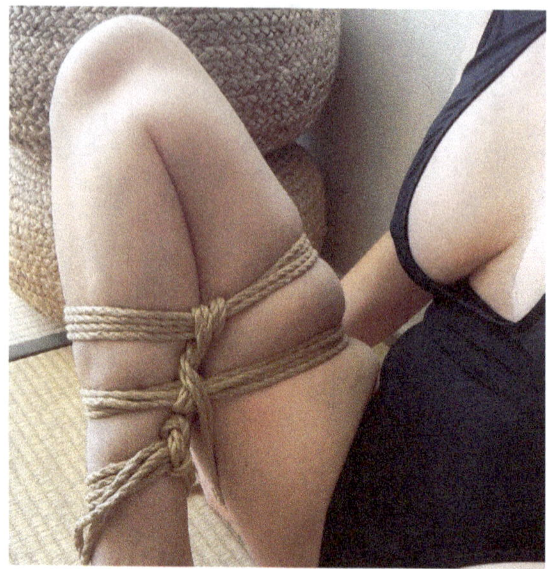

Step 8: Bring the rope through the opening to the outside of the leg.

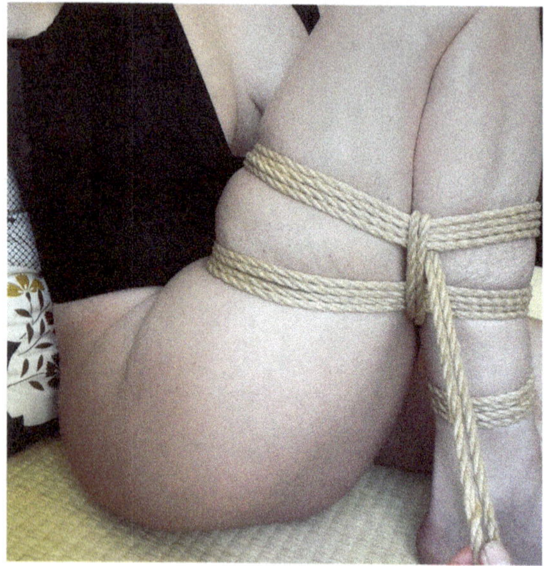

Step 9: Loop around the band that's closest to the knee and pull down to secure it. This prevents the top band from slipping off the knee.

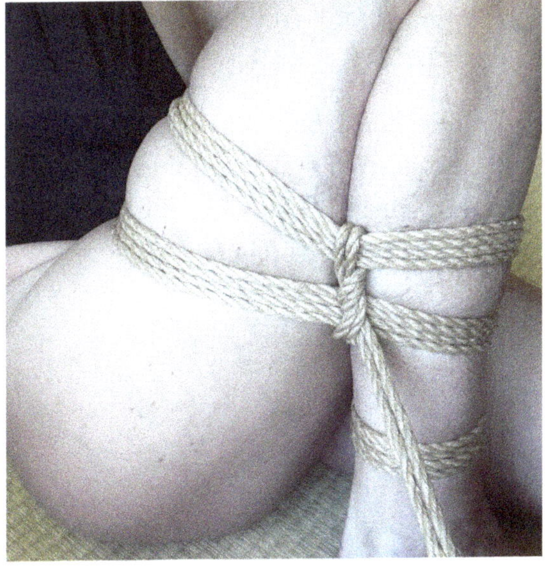

Step 10: Wrap the rope around the stem once. This essentially finishes the tie. All you need to do is to tie-off.

The Futomomo tie can be applied to either just one leg or both legs, depending on the desired outcome and the context of the practice. When tied on a single leg, the Futomomo creates an asymmetrical aesthetic and can be used for specific artistic or functional purposes in Shibari. This method restricts the movement of one leg, often leading to a unique visual appeal and dynamic. You have completed the tie on one leg by following steps 1 - 10 above.

Alternatively, tying the Futomomo on both legs is also common. This approach creates symmetry and can offer a different kind of immobilization and aesthetic. The decision to tie one or both legs is typically based on the preferences and objectives of the individuals involved, as well as the physical comfort and safety of the person being tied.

You now have the option to proceed and replicate the same tie on the other leg.

In Shibari, the choice between one or two legs often depends on the desired emotional and visual impact, as well as practical considerations like the physical capabilities and comfort of the person being tied.

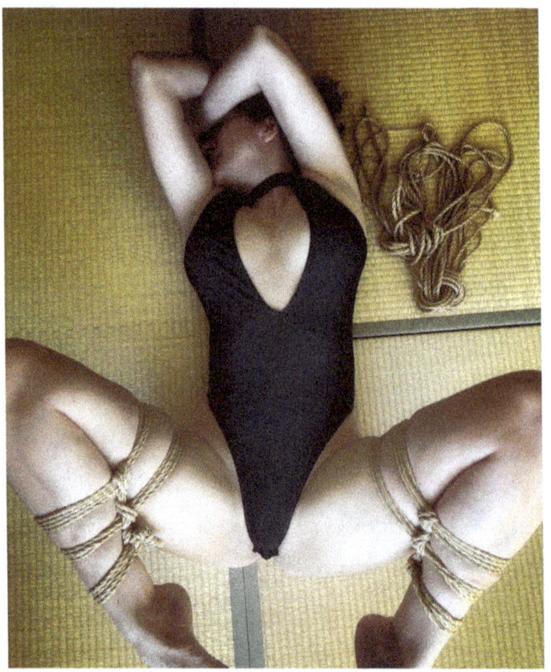

Once you replicate the same tie on both legs, you get to see your partner in a rather enticing predicament.

CONCLUSION

As we conclude our journey through the 'Erotic Art of Shibari,' it's clear that the realms of intimacy and connection we've explored extend far beyond the intricate patterns of rope. I hope that exploring Shibari and learning the five ties detailed in this book has not only enhanced your understanding of intimacy but also deepened your self-awareness and connection with your partner.

As you progress on your path, let each knot and each wrap of rope be a testament to the trust and connection you have nurtured. The techniques and styles explored in these pages are a foundation upon which you can build a more intimate, fulfilling, and connected relationship. Whether exploring a newfound fantasy or enriching an existing bond, the art of Shibari offers a unique canvas for self-expression and discovery.

Carry the lessons and experiences from the 'Erotic Art of Shibari' into your life, and let the ropes guide you to new heights of intimacy, trust, and self-discovery. The journey you've embarked upon doesn't conclude with the last page of this book; it's just the beginning of a deeper exploration into the world of connection and sensual fulfillment. 🚀🧶
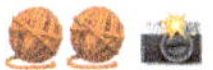🧶🧶📸

ALSO BY THAT ROPE GUY

Knot Tying 101: The Ultimate Beginner's Pocket Guide to 7 Most Useful Knots You Will Ever Need for Shibari

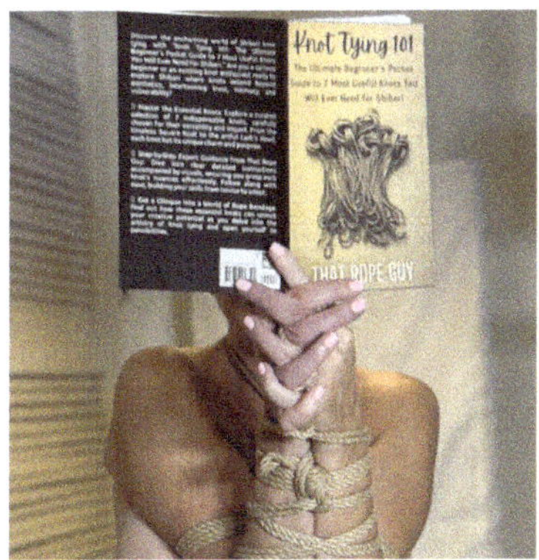

www.ingramcontent.com/pod-product-compliance
Lightning Source LLC
Chambersburg PA
CBHW061431050726
47593CB00006B/2304